# MODERN
# ENGLISH REFORM

## From Individualism to Socialism

*A COURSE OF LOWELL LECTURES*

By

### EDWARD P. CHEYNEY

Professor of History
University of Pennsylvania

Philadelphia
UNIVERSITY OF PENNSYLVANIA PRESS
LONDON: HUMPHREY MILFORD: OXFORD UNIVERSITY PRESS
1931

## CONTENTS

# INTRODUCTION

SPREAD upon the British statute book of the last century and a quarter are some scores, indeed hundreds, of laws of a certain characteristic type. They are laws intended each to remove some particular abuse or to introduce some general improvement in the condition of the people. They are the record of modern English social and political reform. It is the peculiar pride of England that this record is to be found on the statute book, not in the annals of revolution. The process has nevertheless not been an easy one. Back of the passage of each of these laws has been a popular agitation, often a long and bitter contest. Yet the work of reform has gone steadily on. There have been few steps backward; progress has on the whole been constant and stable. In the mass of detailed occurrences there is therefore discoverable a continuous development, the gradual unfolding of a drama, the logical working out of forces inherent in the time. To discover the plot of this drama, to trace this development through the successive stages of British nineteenth and early twentieth century reform is the object of these chapters.

# I

## THE WEALTH AND POVERTY OF ENGLAND IN 1800

AT the beginning of the nineteenth century England was reputed to be, and probably was the wealthiest country of Europe. Its wealth was, in the main, at that time, landed wealth. A favorite form of publication in England is a series of illustrated volumes, "Views of the Estates of Noblemen and Gentlemen," or "Ancient Halls of England and Wales," or "Stately Homes of England." In these handsome volumes are pictured scores, in some series, hundreds of mediaeval or Tudor or Stuart or Georgian "Halls" or "Granges" or "Castles" or "Courts" or "Abbeys" or "Lodges." They are battlemented or pillared or gabled; they crown hilltops, or are built against gently rising slopes, or nestle in valleys. A little river runs through the foreground, or a lake or a pond breaks the smooth extent of lawn stretching away to the park or woods. Trees of inimitable grace and verdure dot the lawns or extend in long avenues or form solid banks of woodland. Cattle, sheep, and deer graze up to the outposts of the gardens; swans float on the water; long-skirted ladies with their children and dogs ramble about, and it is all a scene of beauty, peace, and long established wealth, ease, and refinement. They are indeed the stately homes of England. These castles and country houses of the nobility and gentry, with their outhouses and stables and greenhouses and gardens and parks, were of course of varying degrees of grandeur, but they were all the abodes of comparative wealth.

Supporting them, sometimes in the neighborhood, sometimes at a distance, were broad stretches of farming and forest land. The ownership of the country houses and cultivated lands and profitable forests of England by her nobility and gentry was partly the bequest of the middle ages, partly the plunder of the church during the Reformation, partly the result of three centuries of enclosures of the old open lands of the community. The improvements in agriculture that were in progress were further enriching England and especially this favored class, for their income came, in the main, from the rents paid by their tenant farmers. The high prices of grain in the wars of the French Revolution increased the profitableness of the farms and consequently the rents. It was estimated that between 1790 and 1820 income from rents in England doubled, and agricultural production, according to the census of 1811, amounted in value to about one hundred million pounds or half a billion dollars a year.

This produce of the land must, it is true, support a rather numerous body of reasonably well-to-do tenant farmers and a mass of agricultural laborers, as well as the wealthy landed aristocracy, but the visible, accumulated, and disposable wealth of the countryside was in its country houses and cultivated lands, forests, and meadows connected with them. It was these that gave its special character and appearance to rural England and that were the wonder and admiration of foreign and city visitors. It was in them that dwelt that leisurely class that still lives in the books of Jane Austen, the Brontës, Miss Edgeworth, Miss Burney and other novelists of the early century. Largely parasitic as they were, living on the labors of the classes below them, except for a few who paid for their comfort by estate management, public service, or private philanthropy, and unprofitable as was generally the life of routine and rather vapid social intercourse they lived, they were nevertheless the recipients of a vast income and the possessors of an unrivalled heritage of rural wealth. They were the ancient and solid foundation of the wealth of England. Their income was momentarily threatened by the fall of the price of grain at the close of the Napoleonic wars, but landholders were still supreme in Parliament as they were in the country, so the corn laws were passed, the price of wheat stabilized at something near $2.50 a bushel, and their wealth remained unshattered.

Some landowners had recently been still further enriched by the discovery and development of coal mines below the surface of their lands. Such families as the Lowthers in Westmoreland the Curwens in Cumberland, the Percys in Northumberland, the Bridgewaters in Lancashire, had found in the new demand for an old product, often lying under lands otherwise of relatively small value, enormous additions to their own wealth and that of England. The product of other mines—iron, lead, copper, tin— added some millions to the national income, though it did not usually pass through the hands of so high a social class. Nor was the wealth drawn from the land all preserved in the country. Many of the nobility and gentry had in London or in the county towns, either in their own possession or in the hands of other members of their families, town houses containing furnishings and other accompaniments of luxurious living that compared favorably with the great country houses. The close connection between rural and town wealth is one of the characteristics of England.

The sea has its harvests as well as the land and for more than four centuries importing and exporting merchants of England had been amassing wealth in the form of ships and warehouses and goods in transit and personal property and actual money in use. The time had not yet come, though it was well on its way, when Kipling could write:

Oh, where are you going to, all you Big Steamers,
With England's own coal up and down the salt seas?
We are going to fetch you your bread and your
    butter,
Your beef, pork and mutton, eggs, apples and cheese.

4

And where will you fetch it from, all you Big
　　Steamers,
And where shall I write you when you are away?
We fetch it from Melbourne, Quebec, and Van-
　　couver,
Address us at Hobart, Hong-Kong, and Bombay.

The middle ages had created but little mercantile
wealth, but with the overseas urge of the sixteenth
century and the formation of the great commercial
companies—the Muscovy, the Levant, the East
India, the Hudson Bay—and the appearance of enterprising, individual merchants and partnerships,
a group of rich commercial families was formed
which rivalled in their wealth the older landed
families. The commercial wars of the eighteenth
century and the growth of the colonies gave them
more than equal advantages in the acquisition of
wealth with the increased rents of the landholders.
They lived in houses as extensive, as luxurious, and
filled with even more handsome furniture and richer
plate than all but the very greatest of the landowners. They were able to go beyond them in expenditure, and had at the same time their more
mobile wealth, government loans, stock in trade,
and money in the bank for further adventuring.
The population of London passed the million mark
in 1801 and there were whole streets and suburbs of
wealthy or well-to-do city men. Other towns had
their successful merchant population. Sir John Glad-
tone, father of the statesman, was a typical importing merchant of Liverpool. The merchants of that

city in the year 1800 imported a quarter of a million
pounds of raw cotton, and this was relatively a new
trade. Exports of woolen goods and iron manufactures and imports of furs, tobacco, timber, wheat,
and a score of other products were older and
scarcely less profitable objects of commerce. Liverpool's unenviable primacy in the slave trade added
greatly to her wealth. In the decade 1783–1793, her
merchants carried something over 300,000 slaves
from Africa to the West Indies, and one of them,
Mayor Thomas Leyland, was said to have earned
some $200 per head on those carried on his vessels.
Liverpool was scarcely an exceptional commercial
town. Of Bristol, Hull, Plymouth, and a score of
other ports the same story could be told. Commerce
had created approximately as much wealth for England as agriculture, and the towns were together
probably as rich as the country.

A by-product of commerce was the group of
"nabobs," men who had acquired wealth in the
colonies through the exploitation of the natives or
native resources and had brought that wealth home
with them to utilize and enjoy in either town or
country life. Nor was wealth acquired by trading
restricted to merchant princes. A substantial amount
was distributed among smaller merchants and dealers, down to the shopkeepers of London and the
provincial towns.

England was also a capitalist country. There were
rich banking as well as landed and merchant families. This saved-up and disposable wealth had come

originally largely from trade, but it was now possessed, handled, and increased by bankers. Many of these were or had been Quakers, such as Sir John Barnard and Samuel Gurney of Norwich, founder of the house of Overend and Gurney, or they were Scotchmen, such as Coutts and Company, originally grain dealers of Edinburgh, and Henry Hope, who died a millionaire in 1811. Or they were Jews, like Ricardo and Meyer Rothschild, who came from Germany to England in 1800. There were also numberless wholesale merchant-capitalists who increased the numbers of the well-to-do, and whose fortunes, large and small, helped make up the total of England's wealth.

But perhaps the most significant form of wealth in England at the beginning of the century, certainly the form increasing most rapidly, was that which arose from manufactures. A new and more productive industrial life was then in the heyday of its growth. Regions not before thickly populated or highly cultivated or suitable for commerce were now coming to be dotted with factory chimneys and crowded with manufacturing towns. The formerly less permeable and populous North of England was being rapidly seamed with canals and turnpike roads and was soon to be traversed in all directions by railroads. Newly invented machinery, a new organization of industry, new application of capital, a new opportunity for enterprise and new methods of transportation were rapidly transforming masses of raw material into valuable products. The Industrial

Revolution was in full progress. A chance report of
the year 1788 speaks of one hundred and fifty-three
factories recently built near Manchester. Arthur
Young mentions a new mill costing a sum equal to
$500,000, another twice as much, and still another
three times as much. The first canal, built for the
Duke of Bridgewater, cost $1,000,000; the canals
in existence at the beginning of the century were
estimated to have increased the wealth of England
by $25,000,000. This new industrial equipment was
in the hands largely of a new group of men. The
Arkwrights, Dales, Peels, Brights, Ashtons, Strutts,
Owens, Wedgwoods, and hundreds of others were
fast becoming a new and wealthy aristocracy, destined to power, political recognition, and eventually
to social equality with the older wealthy classes.

Statistics are seldom accurate and there are special difficulties in calculating total wealth and income. But a careful estimate places the total wealth
of England at this time at about a billion and a half
pounds or seven and a half billion dollars, and her
total income at an amount equalling about one and
a half billion dollars. The government had been
able to borrow as much as one and a quarter billion
dollars, through loans for war purposes between
1793 and 1800. Less formal methods of gaining an
impression of the wealth of the country and of the
well-to-do classes are at hand. Miss Burney's Cecilia
was left a fortune of £10,000 a year by her father
though he was a mere private country gentleman
Shirley, though a plain little Yorkshire heiress, has

8

£1000 a year, a fine old house and a dozen servants. Contemporary mention of money, whether as investments in business, subscriptions to charities, or gambling gains and losses, is always in large sums. Contemporary pictures of men and women of the upper classes whether at meetings of Parliament, public assemblies, Ranelagh Gardens, the Derby, city clubs, or rural inns, show handsomely dressed groups, spending freely, eating luxuriously and living a leisurely life.

The expenditure of one of the newest of the rich men of England may be guessed from the following contemporary description. "On Sunday last Sir Rich. Arkwright, Knt. High Sheriff of the county, arrived at Derby accompanied by a great number of gentlemen on horseback; his javelin men, thirty in number, dressed in the richest liveries ever seen there on such an occasion, all rode on black horses. The trumpeters were mounted on gray horses and elegantly dressed in scarlet and gold. The High Sheriff's coach was very elegant and fashionable, with plated furnishings. etc."

Such was the wealthy England of 1800; endowed with her great accumulations from the past, rich in native resources, her factories pouring out valuable products, her harbors filled with ships, her roads and canals crowded with goods, her farms and mines productive, her people enterprising and industrious. What a wealthy country is England! Such is the irresistible exclamation of the onlooker. There must be plenty for all. So rich a country must be able to give to all her people comfort, if not luxury. We have enumerated class after class of the population who were holders of property and receivers of a liberal income. If there are other classes not so fortunate, the national income will certainly hold out to give them sustenance and provide their fundamental needs.

To test the adequacy of this judgment an effort may be made to estimate the proportionate numbers of the classes of the British people a century ago. No exactitude is of course possible and these numbers may be little more than guesswork. They may serve nevertheless to illustrate a point which is in itself indubitable. In a recent topographical work four chance counties disclose respectively seventy-five, something over a hundred, a hundred and fifty, and two hundred and twenty gentlemen's seats with names of some antiquity. If therefore an average of two hundred landed estates in each county may be taken as a fair estimate we would have some 10,000 families of the landed nobility and gentry. There may have been some 8000 substantial merchants in London and 2000 in other towns. There were perhaps 2000 financial personages of weight and wealth. The new cotton manufacturers, ironmasters and others manufacturing on a large enough scale to join in a national organization numbered about 5000. Successful professional men, lawyers, physicians, officers in the army and navy, and holders of lucrative offices under the national government or the governments of towns, perhaps added up to 3000 more. Of churchmen, the twenty-five bishops, one hundred and fifty canons and others on a list of holders of the better church offices made up, perhaps, more than 1000.

This makes some 30,000 individuals or, with their families, about 150,000 persons. The population of England in 1801 was 8,750,000. That is, the enumerated classes of the actually wealthy were about one-sixtieth of the population. We have discussed this one-sixtieth, what was the position of the other fifty-nine sixtieths? Of the seven and a half billions of property or the one and a half billions of income that made England so wealthy a country, what proportion went to the hundred and fifty thousand, what proportion to the eight million six hundred thousand? It is true that there must have been large numbers hardly to be included in the wealthy— the farmers, the lower clergy, small shopkeepers, petty office-holders, teachers, clerks, persons living on small savings, who formed a not unprosperous middle class. These must be considered as modest possessors of some humble share of England's wealth. But how many they were we have no statistics to furnish even a basis for guessing. The rich were few, the middle classes may have been many.

Let us however give up the almost futile effort to estimate relative numbers and wealth and turn to look at English society from the bottom instead of from the top. A suggestive anecdote of the prime minister is given by a diarist of 1795. "Mr. Pitt, being on a visit in Essex descanted with great satisfaction on the prosperous state of the country. His host let the discourse drop, but contrived that on the following day Mr. Pitt should walk in the adjoining town of Halsted. It presented a state of the utmost poverty and wretchedness. He surveyed it in wonder and silence, and then declared that he had no conception that England presented in any part of it such a scene." In 1812 Lord Byron, just returned from the Orient and speaking for the first time in the House of Lords, declared, doubtless with some exaggeration, but with sincere feeling, "I have been in some of the most oppressed provinces of Turkey, but never under the most despotic infidel governments did I behold such squalid wretchedness as I have seen since my return in the very heart of a Christian country. I have seen men meagre with famine, sullen with despair, careless of life." In the same year a government official, speaking in Parliament in favor of a bill for training poor boys for the navy says he can readily secure 90,000 boys of the proper age for the purpose from the poorhouses of the country. Another official writes, somewhat later, concerning Manchester, "The streets of this town are horrible. The poor starving people go about in twenties and forties begging." As such testimony piles up it becomes evident that there is much in England besides wealth and besides even the comfort of the middle classes.

Not only the amount of property but the contrast between the wealth and the poverty of the country impressed contemporaries. Greville in his journal, describing the first outbreak of cholera, in the third decade of the century, remarks, "The awful thing is the vast extent of misery and distress which prevails and the evidence of the rotten foundation on which the whole fabric of this gorgeous society rests; for I call that rotten which exhibits thousands upon thousands of human beings reduced to the lowest stage of moral and physical degradation, with no more of the necessaries of life than serve to keep body and soul together, whole classes of artisans without the means of subsistence— Extremes prevail of the most unbounded luxury and enjoyment and the most dreadful privation and suffering." Or, again, describing a trial at the Old Bailey, "The case exhibited a shocking scene of wretchedness and poverty such as ought not to exist in any community, especially in one which pretends to be so flourishing and happy as this." Baroness Lieven, the observant wife of the Russian ambassador, remarks, "The aristocracy rolls in wealth and luxury, while the streets of London and the highways of the country swarm with miserable creatures covered with rags, barefooted, having neither food nor shelter." General Sir Charles Napier, destined always to sympathize with the poor but to command the troops who protected the rich, writes bitterly to his mother in 1816, "There are two million of people in England starving to enable Lord Camden to receive £38,000 a year and to spend it on game and other amusements." And, again, "The English poor may speak with bated breath of the wealth of their country, but they are not to get the smallest taste of it." And, "the Irish laborer looks at the rasher of bacon suspended above his table but eats only his potatoes."

An American visitor points out that "the condition of the lower classes at the present moment is a mournful comment on English institutions and civilization. The multitude are depressed in that country to a degree of ignorance, want and misery which must touch every heart not made of stone. In the civilized world there are few sadder spectacles than the present contrast in Great Britain of unbounded wealth and luxury with the starvation of thousands and tens of thousands, crowded into cellars and dens, without ventilation or light, compared with which the wigwam of the Indian is a palace. Misery, famine, brutal degradation, in the presence of stately mansions which ring with gaiety and dazzle with pomp and unbounded profusion."

"The distress of the people" is one of the most familiar expressions in parliamentary debate. It might well be so. In 1801 about one and a quarter million of the eight and three quarter millions of the population, one in seven, are receiving poor relief; in Birmingham this rises to one in three. In Drury Lane district in London 3000 of the 5000 families live in one room. In another London district, "It is a fortunate family which has one room to itself." "Orchard Place is less than 45 yards long and 8 broad and contains 27 homes. Residents in the court in 1845 were no less than 217 families, consisting of 882 persons." In Liverpool the cellar houses, of which there are 6284, are 10 or 12 feet square generally flagged, but frequently having only the bare earth for a floor and sometimes less than 6 feet in height. There is frequently no window, so that light and air can gain access to the cellar only by the door, the top of which is often not higher than the level of the street. There are few cellars where at least two families do not herd together."

This is in the town. According to a long series of reports the country is worse. In one county "The majority of the cottages are wretchedly built, often in very unhealthy sites; they are miserably small and are crowded to excess, they are very low, seldom drained, and badly roofed; and they scarcely ever have any cellar or space under the floor of the lower rooms. The floors are formed either of flags, which rest upon the cold, undrained ground, or, as is often the case, of nothing but a mixture of clay and lime." Statements from country clergymen, sanitary authorities, agents of landlords, and other observers describe in village after village, in shire after shire, the miserable dwellings of the peasantry, whole families and groups of both sexes, "pigging" together in the same room, often in the same bed, filthy, immoral, illiterate, debased beyond modern realization, almost beyond belief. Bastardy is so common as to seem, as it doubtless was, a normal accompaniment of the way of living of the farm laborers of England. And again the same contrast between riches and poverty. These miserable dwelling places of the mass of the rural population lay often on the very confines of the parks of the gentry.

Even in fiction appears as a background to the life of the fashionable and well-to-do, ever and anon, the misery of the poor. It is true that the country swains and their lasses and the lavender-sellers and the working men and women and their children in the contemporary paintings of Morland and Bonington, Crome and Gainsborough and even Constable are well dressed and comfortable looking, but this is due to the exigencies of the palette or the dictates of romance. The moment realism asserts itself we have the barbarities of Hogarth and the sordid descriptions of Crabbe. Wherever in contemporary record, whether statistics, diaries, speeches, literature, or art, the decent veil of romance, convention or complacence is drawn aside, we see masses of the English people spending their lives in the deepest poverty, privation, ignorance and neglect.

What a poverty-stricken country is England! Such is now the exclamation of the observer. The evidence for her poverty is as overwhelming as is that for her wealth. There are two Englands. One is the England of the upper classes, the fortunate, the rich and comfortable; the other is the England of the masses. Only by shutting eyes and ears to the testimony for the one can we accept the other as the real England. Both are real. "The riches and the poverty of the land" is the biblical formula. It is an ancient contrast. For some reason it was especially true that in England dire poverty coexisted with great wealth. It is not an illusion or a mistake, but a plain historical fact that England was at the beginning of the nineteenth century a marvellously rich country, in which, due to some fatal maladjustment, poverty was rampant and need the general condition of the mass of the people. The causes for this contrast might be inquired into, but it is not they but the action to which the contrast led that is the subject of this book.

One may be justified, in the interests of optimism, in interrupting the narrative for a moment to call attention to the disappearance of many of these conditions from modern England. Poverty still exists, problems remain to be solved, there is much that is unsatisfactory, even deplorable, in modern English society, but there is no longer starvation, raggedness, cellar-living, except by some tragic and occasional mischance. Sad enough sights and exigencies there are now, as any inquirer may learn, but the worst sights noticeable at every turn a century ago and testified to by innumerable witnesses, are no longer to be found in England by any student of social conditions, native or foreign.

There is just one other consideration which might modify our judgment upon that time. Were the conditions of distress general or were they merely local or casual or restricted to the thriftless and drunken? This question can be tested with some accuracy. In the year 1801 there were food riots in Sheffield in the north, Norwich in the east, Brighton in the south, Worcester in the west and Coventry and Nottingham in the midlands. Destitution in that year was evidently not local. Again, restriction and even privation might exist, yet without actual distress except in certain contingencies. That is a matter of the standard of life, of wages compared with prices, and of regularity of employment. Were ordinary wages adequate for comfort and health? Lists of wages and prices are abundant. For instance, according to a government accounting in the year 1800, daily wages of mechanics at Greenwich were, for plumbers 3s 3d, carpenters 3s 2d, bricklayers 3s, masons 2s 10d. These, reduced to more familiar units, amount to about $5 a week for the highest, $4.10 for the lowest. In the same year Arthur Young reports agricultural laborers in a large part of England as receiving 9s per week as wages and 6s from the poor rates, equalling together about $3.75 a week. Millworkers in Glasgow at the same time were receiving about $5 a week, miners from $4 to $5.10. Journeymen tailors, about the highest paid operatives, when regularly at work could earn 24s, equalling about $6.00 weekly. A great number of other instances, though showing much variation do not reach higher nor, under normal circumstances, fall appreciably lower than this. Wages of men, therefore, might be considered to extend from about $3.50 to $5 a week. Women's wages were from $1.25 to $3 per week.

These of course were nominal not real wages. What about prices? A list of food prices in the Annual Register for 1801, transformed into American figures, is as follows: meat 18¢ per lb., cheese 8¢ per lb., butter 35¢ per lb., tea 60¢ per lb., sugar 35¢ per lb., bread from 5¢ to 8¢ per lb. according to changes in the price of grain. Of these it is obvious that meat, butter and cheese are lower than present English or American prices, tea and sugar are higher, bread is on the average about the same. It is evident that bread could not be cheap with wheat rising frequently to $2.50, $3.00 or even $4.00 a bushel, though there was a quicker response in the food market to its fall then than now. Rent, clothing, leather and some metal goods were cheaper than in modern times, but not very much cheaper. From these and a large number of other calculations one reaches the conclusion that the cost of living was lower but not greatly lower than in modern times, whereas wages were very much lower. Recent authoritative calculations have placed the real value of present prevailing English wages at four times their value at the beginning of last century. To the present writer that seems unduly favorable to modern wages. But in any case the standard of life of the whole working class was in 1800 a very low one. Distress was not only in times of disaster, and poverty was the lot not of the unfortunate and incompetent only. There was an immeasurable hiatus between the usual habits of living of the upper and the lower classes and but a narrow margin between the usual wages of the latter and actual suffering.

Then, as now, it was the irregularity of employment that was the greatest source of distress. Any fall from a standard that barely supported life, a crisis in trade and consequent discharge or cutting down of wages, a bad harvest and consequent rise of the price of food, brought a great part of the population into utter misery. The depression in business of the early years of the century threw great numbers out of work and caused a cut in wages. In 1806 weavers at Broughton were getting only $2.60 a week, in 1819 ironworkers in Wales were getting only $1.50 a week and factory workers in Glasgow $1.30. The poor law of England, hard worked as it was, had been intended for the support of a relatively small class of permanent paupers; it was not adjusted to the requirements of an increasingly industrialized population with frequent temporary loss of occupation. So bad times and business failures were reflected immediately in an increase of deplorable poverty. At any one time some hundreds of thousands of the artisans and working classes of England occupied at their usual wages were living on a level of bare subsistence; down below them were a mass of men, women and children, permanently or temporarily underpaid, underfed, ill clothed, living in congested quarters, ignorant, miserable, and drunken. Prevailing wages, prices, and irregularity of occupation taken into consideration therefore, it is a fact that a great part of the English people were a sodden and unhappy and restless mass, compared with whose condition

he wealth of England seems as we look back on it
an absurd anomaly or a cruel jest of fate.

This is a sombre story, too sombre perhaps as here
old, for actuality. There were doubtless cases of
comfort and content; there must have been groups
and individuals not in the specially privileged
classes who were nevertheless more favorably situ-
ated than others. Too many men rose from the lower
classes to permit the belief that the case of those
classes was hopeless; many who made the best of a
bad job evidently found it endurable. Humanity
has great capacity for survival. Yet a careful judgment, no matter how forbearing, based upon contemporary testimony, must be a harsh one.

The description of England a century or more
ago, as so far given, has been of her material condition. It is conceivable that her political, religious,
and intellectual wealth was better distributed. Let
us see! Englishmen were inheritors of a great con-
stitutional tradition of freedom and self-government. England was apparently as wealthy a nation
politically as materially. Montesquieu, perhaps not
too well informed, had set her government before
the Continent as a model. Burke, the greatest of her
own political philosophers, treated the English constitution as something sacred, hallowed by age, its
authority justified by its internal excellence. The
Duke of Wellington in a famous speech in Parliament declared that if he were asked to make a form
of government for any country he would copy that

of England as closely as possible. Even yet there are writers who look back to her government at this period as a particularly excellent government. At first sight there seems some justification for such a contemporary and modern estimate. The English people were in a certain sense a free people. Parliament, the national assembly, was supreme. It was Parliament, not a king, that controlled taxation, made statutes, even to a considerable degree directed diplomatic relations and decided upon war and peace. England was "a republic with a crown in its 'scutcheon." It might seem that the English people ruled themselves, and there were some who declared that they ruled themselves well.

Yet in the realm of government as in more material fields, there is other testimony. Shelley was not a careful observer, but there were others more moderate and more competent who yet agreed with his bitter description of the government written in the second decade of the century.

"An old, mad, blind, despised and dying king,
  Princes, the dregs of their dull race—
  Rulers who neither see, nor feel, nor know,
  But leech-like to their fainting country cling.
  A people starved and stabbed in the untilled field,
  Golden and sanguine laws which tempt and slay—
  A senate—Time's worst statute unrepealed."

It is the government, not economic society that Place described as "this old rotten system." Indeed contemporary criticism meets us at every turn. The incapacity and corruption of government are

he constant objects of complaint and the familiar
butt of the wit of the time. Moreover we have the
same contrast between the political as between the
economic wealth of the few and poverty of the
many. All the self government, all the parliamentary control, all office, was the monopoly of an
extremely small part of the people. All political
power and most political advantage was in the
possession of but one hundred or two hundred or
perhaps three hundred thousand of the eight and
three quarters millions of the people. The upper
classes were politically privileged, the lower classes
had neither part nor lot in the matter. All members
of Parliament and voters for them, all judges and
magistrates and those who influenced their selec-
tion, all officers in the army and navy, all ambas-
sadors and other foreign representatives, all administrative officials, were selected from the few
hundred thousands of the ruling class. If not more
than one out of sixty belonged to the well-to-do
classes, scarcely more belonged to the politically
ruling classes. It was in the year 1800 that as moderate a statesman as Pitt expressed the aristocratic
ideal of government when he said, "There may be
occasions, but they will ever be few, when an appeal
to the people is the just mode of proceeding on important subjects." This political condition is described as follows by a modern English historian
far from lacking in admiration for the institutions
of his native country: "In the generation following
1792 Britain was not a free country. The island was

governed by a certain number of privileged persons
and the bulk of the inhabitants not only had n
share of any sort in the government, but they wer
debarred from demanding a share by laws especiall
enacted for this purpose and savagely admin
istered." Modern admiration for the old aristocrati
government of England is misapplied.

It is a suggestive thought that the views on polit
ical policy expressed by Burke, Fox, Pitt, Grey
Wilberforce, and other parliamentary leaders ar
not differences of ideas among the English peopl
but only personal opinions of one very small sec
tion of the English people. They were at best dis
putes among the members of a political clique. T
find the opinions of the English nation it would b
necessary to go much further afield.

Contemporary criticism was however not onl
of the narrowness but of the incompetence of th
government of the time. Was the political wealt
of England real wealth, like her material posse
sions, even though in the hands of a few, or was
sham wealth? Horace Walpole called the Hous
of Lords "a mob of nobility." In the sixty year
from 1760 to 1820, three hundred and eighty-eigl
new peerages had been created in a House of Lor
of about six hundred. These were mostly "ne
men," and, due to the exigencies of politics, were a
most all Tories. These in turn controlled the ele
tion of more than one half of the House of Con
mons, which was consequently almost solidly Tor
As a result a great many incapable men were i

cluded, a great many able men, members by birth
and position of the ruling class, were excluded from
Parliament because of their political views. Sidney
Smith said "It was an awful time for those who
had the misfortune to entertain liberal opinions."
The same party spirit and favoritism extended to
appointments, which were but seldom based on
ability. The Tory government was but a poor embodiment of its own ideal of government by a class
trained to power and responsibility. It was under
constant and sharp criticism by the Whig party,
which was not fundamentally less aristocratic. It
was inefficient, faced periodically with half-mutiny
in the army and navy, and constantly with what Pitt
described in a letter to Addington as the "progress
of discontent and internal mischief."

Legislation was largely class legislation. Game
laws to gratify landowners, penal laws to protect
each special form of property, combination acts to
strengthen employers against the nascent trade
unions, gave testimony to the class consciousness
of Parliament and its preoccupation with the defense of the interests of its own members. Above
all was the constant struggle of the ministers to
gain or retain office. English political life often re-
minds one of boys playing a game. It is all so
personal, so earnest, directed so single-mindedly to
success, either of the individual or of his side, so
respectful of precedent. It is true the game they
play is the game of empire. The questions they debate, the problems they endeavor to settle are in

many cases so serious that they must needs use high argument. This is, as it were, in spite of themselves; the natural attitude of English statesmen in contending for ministerial office is none the less that of contestants on the ball field.

England during this period fought a victorious war against France and Napoleon, but it was in the midst of bitter criticism of the government, disunion among classes and individuals, and at an enormous economic, financial, and moral cost. Such an incompetent and ill-supported government in the crisis of a century later would have invited and suffered early defeat. Thus, not only was the political wealth of England monopolized by a few, but that wealth itself was of doubtful value. No phase of existing society in England at the beginning of our period was more vulnerable to criticism and attack than its political phase.

England had a wealthy established church; rich in endowments, privileges, and prestige. Its bishops were members of the House of Lords and thus participated in government; its lower clergy were frequently magistrates and always influential in affairs of the civil parish, and therefore participants in local administration. The piety of past ages had provided a vast number of foundations for education, charity, and religion, and far the greater number of these were in charge of the established church. The clergy were usually well-educated and refined and some of them realized their duties and utilized their opportunities. But all material favors

of the church were for a small minority of the
people. The body of the clergy were drawn almost
entirely from the group of families which monopolized landed and commercial wealth and political
power. It would be an exaggeration to deny to the
established church a modicum of influence over the
people of England, especially over the more backward and stolid elements. It is also true that there
are saints in all countries and times. A goodly number of learned and pious churchmen can be named
as living in 1800, and many devoted souls whose
names are forgotten were doubtless giving to their
parishioners such comfort and help as the church
offered and their own good sense dictated. Nevertheless it is in the main true that the church of England at the beginning of the nineteenth century,
however well-endowed and firmly established, was
quite undevout and largely sterile.

Its endowments were looked upon primarily as a
source of support for the younger sons of the nobility and gentry. That the oldest son should inherit
the land, the second go into the army and the third
into the church was well established custom. When
the hero of *Sense and Sensibility,* presumptive heir
to lands worth £1000 a year, is cut off from his
inheritance, he immediately decides to be ordained
and accepts the offer of a friendly neighboring
landlord of a rectory worth £200 a year. His scape-
grace brother, who now becomes heir of the land,
laughs loudly at the idea of his brother in a sur-
plice publishing banns, while another neighbor

27

wonders that the patron should have given away a living which he could have sold for £1400. It is no wonder a pious character in *Shirley* exclaims, "God save the church—and God reform it." Indeed the part the church plays in contemporary fiction is its most effective if unconscious condemnation. The devotion of the masses to the church was restricted largely to "church and king," and "no popery" propaganda. From the religious and moral point of view its influence over the common people and its service to them were practically nil. Their religious life, so far as it showed any vitality, gathered around Dissent or Methodism. Deism was widespread in the upper classes, plain religious ignorance in the lowest. The Methodist and Evangelical revival had aroused much religious fervor in certain restricted groups, and the Quakers and Unitarians were interesting themselves in works of practical piety. Apart from these England, from a religious point of view, was not wealthy but poor.

In the field of the intellect an age and a nation which offered to the world so large a number of men and women productive in fiction, poetry, history, science, criticism, and all other forms of mental activity, a land where culture was so widespread and the mind of man so free, can with difficulty be subjected to an adverse judgment, or even to question. Yet it is astonishing on what a background of popular ignorance all this was projected. Opportunities for education, apart from individual effort, were incredibly restricted. The old universities

with their rich colleges, the public schools and
larger endowed schools were utilized for the education, such as it was, of the same small section of
the people we have already so often met in the seats
of privilege. In the smaller endowed and grammar
schools, a few schools carried on for profit, and in
still fewer cathedral and denominational schools a
larger representation of the middle classes found
their few opportunities for education. Some of the
rich had private tutors. For the lower classes there
were practically no provisions. "The poor of England are . . . very much worse educated than the
poor of any other European nation, solely except-
ing Russia, Turkey, South Italy, Portugal and
Spain. . . . About one half of our poor can neither
read nor write. . . . It is a very common thing for
even farmers to sign their names with a cross from
being unable to write. You cannot address one of
them without being at once painfully struck with
the intellectual darkness that enshrouds him." Such
are the concluding sentences of a Master of Arts of
Cambridge sent out by his university to examine
popular education in England and on the Continent.

The type of education given at the various institutions was as unsatisfactory as their number was
inadequate. This was one of the periods of ebb-
tide in the intellectual life of the universities. The
bitter reminiscences of Gibbon in his *Autobiography* may be unfair to his university, but his general indictment of the professors and fellows can
hardly be untrue. They are "decent, easy men who

29

supinely enjoyed the gifts of the founder." . . .
"From the toil of reading or thinking or working
they had absolved their consciences." "Their con-
versation stagnated in a round of college business,
Tory politics, personal anecdote and private scan-
dal."

In the public and large endowed schools, the
boys went through the forms but seldom secured
the actuality of a classical education, though one
of them testifies: "By the common methods of discipline, at the expense of many tears and some
blood, I purchased the knowledge of the Latin syn-
tax." They kept up the tradition of a certain rude
and liberty-loving and in some sense a democratic
life, but it extended for the most part only to their
own class. They were sons of the aristocracy and
had no interest, little fellow-feeling and in fact
little knowledge of any one outside their own social
class. Moreover, their standards were brutal, and
by all testimony, to the gifted or intellectually inclined, public-school life was little less than tor-
ture. The endowments of the smaller schools had
been largely diverted to other purposes and the
actual private schools were generally poor. Of
course mental hunger will satisfy itself if there
is any possibility of finding food, and many an
alert-minded boy gained for himself an education
from books loaned him by some kindly clergyman,
lawyer, or student. Robert Owen and Francis
Place emerged largely because of such opportunities, and one who had much more but scarcely

better schooling testifies with a sudden accession of warmth to his own "early and invincible love of reading, which I would not exchange for the treasures of India." It is one of the great glories of the English intellect that it has survived its educational system.

So it was with the army and navy. There was a high standard of personal honor and courage and patriotism, even if there was but little professional training and but mediocre natural capacity among the officers. But there was an immeasurable chasm between the officers and the common men of either service. Old custom and the system of purchase of commissions put officerships in the hands of the well-to-do and the aristocratic. The natural and no doubt necessary distinction between officers and privates was intensified by the social difference between their respective classes. One officer quite casually indicates this difference. He is describing their quarters in Kent. "Our men have got the opthalmia very badly and are dying fast from inflammation of the lungs, caused by coldness of the weather and bad barracks,—the men die three or four a day; no officer suffers, they are warmer." Army discipline was not only hard but permeated with class favoritism. Sir Robert Wilson tells that in the campaign in Flanders in 1794 it was a common sight to see a court-martial sitting in the morning, the members of which were not yet sober after the debauch of the previous night, condemning private soldiers to 900 lashes for the crime of drunkenness. An officer in 1809 speaks of "the ferocity of a discipline which is a disgrace to civilization," and acknowledges that it was largely for the purpose of securing the subserviency of the men to the officers. It was the outspoken criticism by Cobbett of the flogging of some militia men at Ely in 1809 that led to his fine and imprisonment for two years.

An army is, after all, an instrument adjusted to a special purpose, and such tyranny of officers over men might be justified as a necessity if it had been efficacious in producing a satisfactory military system. It was not so. As one reads in the contemporary records of the gross favoritism in promotions and assignments, the grave imperfections of the army in organization and morale, its terrible failures and sufferings during the Napoleonic wars, no justification can be found in its excellence for its class basis and savage code. It is a military, not a civilian historian who declares in a modern work, "It is difficult to read with patience in the diaries and letters of the subordinate officers the state of military mismanagement that existed at this time.—If men care to know what happened to our army when the press was gagged, when authority strutted its way from blunder to blunder, unchecked by the fear of public censure, they should study the military history of the early years of the century from the rupture of the Peace of Amiens to the campaign of Crimea."

There were some differences between the army and navy. The social prestige of the latter was less.

Men of little birth often rose to high naval command; this seldom if ever occurred in military life. On the other hand, whipping survived in the navy after it had disappeared from the army, and the still greater supremacy of the officers over the men probably more than compensated for any social defect in the naval officers' position. For the men there was the press gang. Common workmen going about their business in or near seaports were apt to be seized by the King's men and forced on shipboard for sea service. This was constantly done notwithstanding the traditions of English liberty. An extract from a Newcastle newspaper of 1812 is characteristic. "Monday near thirty riotous seamen were taken on the Tyne at Shields and lodged safe in his Majesty's ship Transit. The peace of the port has frequently been disturbed under pretense of demanding more wages, but now positive orders are given by the Admiralty to the commanding officer here to impress such lawless hands." Re-enlistment in a condition of drunkenness or desperation was scarcely distinguishable from force and this whole body of debased material was kept under by a savage use of the whip, the irons and, at a pinch, the pistol. The familiar modern poster appealing to young men to enlist in the navy on the grounds of education, opportunity to see the world, smart appearance, and pleasant companionship is about as complete an antithesis between the old and the new as social history affords.

Is it necessary to apply the same analysis to the

judiciary? The judges at Westminister and on circuit, the attorney and solicitor general, the officials of the Chancery and of the courts of common law, the sheriffs and juries, the justices of the peace individually and in petty and quarter sessions made up a famous judicial system which plays a large part in contemporary description and in fiction, as it played in real life. But it is famous for its delays, for the harshness and narrowness of its judgments, rather than for its enlightenment or justice. The traditional conservatism of the law, like the severity in the army and navy, was strengthened by the class feeling and, in local justice, by the personal interests of its administrators. Fear of the lower classes led to strained justice and harsh punishment for any approach to sedition or any criticism of the government. This fear extended to industrial as well as political unrest. The upper classes were in a constant panic for fear of revolution or some kind of violent change, and the courts were their first line of defense. We shall later have occasion to speak of some of the deficiencies of the courts and the savagery of criminal law administered by them. It is enough here to point out that they were the object of severe criticism by philosophical writers of the time and of distrust and hatred on the part of the lower classes. Next to the parliamentary system, the judicial system seemed most to demand reorganization.

So from a far broader than the mere material point of view we have a sharp contrast between the

wealth and the poverty of England. To say that
England was rich in material possessions and in
her principal institutions was true; to say that she
was poor in the same respects was equally true.
There are two traditions of England. The one is
the England of romance, politics, fashion, society,
the favored upper classes, commerce, the new manufactures; the other is the England of statistics,
of the writings of realistic observers, of Hogarth,
of overwhelming contemporary evidence, of the
miserable masses. If any country ever needed and
challenged reform, from the foundation upward,
through its whole structure, it was England at the
beginning of the nineteenth century.

At first sight society seemed stereotyped in its
old form. The limited, self-centered, distrustful
group of the ruling classes, ensconced in wealth,
office, political and economic power, and social
prestige, seemed content to allow the most shocking abuses and grave injustices to remain in existence. Their instincts and their immediate interests were all against change. The Duke of Clarence
once remarked that change of any kind brought
about by any means for any purpose was a bad
thing. This royal nonentity would hardly have been
acknowledged as their spokesman by any considerable number of the people of England, but his attitude was only too prevalent; things had best remain
as they were. Yet it is obvious that such a condition of affairs, subjected to the attrition of a critical age, affected by new economic forces and acted

upon perhaps by still deeper influences, could not remain unchanged. That the change was in the direction of improvement was doubtless due to that sum of human influences that usually works toward progress. As a matter of fact the reforms that were so badly needed were in the course of time measurably achieved, and they were achieved, as reforms must always be, from within, and by effort. Who the reformers were, what obstacles they met, and what methods they adopted to overcome them will be the subject of the next chapter.

## II

## THE REFORMERS AND THEIR
## METHODS, 1796–1846

IF England at the beginning of the nineteenth
century needed reform, its germs were already
there; if she needed reformers they were not lacking. Imbedded in the apparently static society of the
time were many centers of infection, as they must
have been considered by conservatives wedded to
things as they were. Even in the midst of high
aristocratic society were individuals and groups
thoroughly dissatisfied with existing conditions and
desirous of more or less extensive changes. There
was, for instance, the so-called "Clapham Sect."
Between 1790 and 1820 or later, one might frequently have found gathered around the dinner
table or in the drawing room or library of one or
other of their number a group of friends, most of
whom lived or had town houses or rooms in the
suburb of Clapham, southwest of London. It was an
interesting and distinguished circle. The one whose
dining room or library was perhaps their most frequent gathering place was Henry Thornton, son of
a London banker, without profession except for his
literary, social, and philanthropic interests and

his membership for many years in the House of Commons. William Wilberforce, a Yorkshire land-owner, wealthy and aristocratic and also a member of Parliament, who spent much of his time at a dwelling bequeathed to him by an uncle in Clapham, was destined to the widest and most enduring fame. Charles Grant, one of the "nabobs," formerly an official in India and now chairman of the Court of Directors of the East India Company in London, also rich and from 1802 to 1818 a member of Parliament, was a frequent participant in the society and discussions of the group. In 1802 another Anglo-Indian, John Shore, formerly governor-general of India and a friend of Warren Hastings, lately made Lord Teignmouth and thus a member of the House of Lords, came to Clapham to live. Others were socially less prominent. Thomas Clarkson, a well-to-do country gentleman, was a frequent visitor to Wilberforce; Granville Sharp, a lawyer; John Bowdler, the expurgator of Shakespeare; Zachary Macaulay, the father; and Thomas Babington, the uncle, of the historian; John Venn, the rector of the parish whose church most of them attended; and more occasional visitors made up an interesting and influential group.

They evidently sought and enjoyed one another's company. They were all cultured, widely read and interested in literature, almost all rich, several of them members of Parliament, and all but two or three Tories in politics. That which seems most to have held them together was the fact that they were all "Evangelicals," devout and strict church-men though not especially interested in the church as a sacramental organization. They were rather ridiculed by friends not closely connected with their group and called "the Saints" or, as already intimated, the "Clapham Sect."

An equally strong bond among them and that which gives them special interest here is their sympathetic attitude and in some cases their whole-hearted devotion to good works. They were gener-ous givers of time and money to philanthropic ob-jects. It is recorded of Thornton that he gave six-sevenths of his income before his marriage and one-third of it afterward to charities and philan-thropies. They were all interested in the reform of Parliament, the extension of public education, the improvement of public morals, the alleviation of poverty, and perhaps most generally and actively, at the beginning of the century, in the abolition of the slave trade. |The names of Wilberforce, Clark-son, Zachary Macaulay, and Granville Sharp are al-most synonymous with that famous agitation of which something more in detail will be said later. But all these men might be counted on to respond favorably to humanitarian proposals and as a mat-ter of fact these engaged most of their interest and efforts.|It must of course be remembered that they were of aristocratic position and training, that not too much trust in the lower classes or lower-class movements must be expected from them, and that some of them in political fields were reactionaries rather than reformers.

Across the Thames, and in a somewhat more modest region socially, in Queen's Square, Westminster, lived Jeremy Bentham. Under his influence at this period was a group of men similar in many of their interests, yet strangely contrasted in their religion and politics, with those who have just been named. Jeremy Bentham was a man of independent means, learned, philosophical, fertile of new ideas, and industrious, but hopelessly obscure as a writer. His *Introduction to the Principles of Morals and Legislation* was written in 1775, published in 1788, translated into French and republished in 1802. But in none of these forms did it secure readers. During these twenty-five and more years of obscurity he wrote and published also many lesser essays, in which he formulated a complete philosophy of human society, a science of human nature. Expressions that later became familiar coin of conversational intercourse or watchwords of party, and ideas that have become common property are to be found imbedded in the writing and thinking of Bentham, such as "general utility," "the greatest happiness of the greatest number," "the search for pleasure and the avoidance of pain," "emancipation from the past," "the exclusive test of right and wrong,—the tendency of actions to produce pleasure or pain," and "the perfectibility of the world." All this philosophy however remained unknown and unread until, after about 1808, the friendship and assistance of James Mill, a clear-thinking and clear-writing young Scotchman, and the gradual aggregation of a group of friends, visitors, and correspondents, reinterpreted and applied the fertile ideas of Bentham to the times. Sir James Romilly, the banker and economist Ricardo, Francis Place, the tailor, and James Hume, the Radical, met and conversed and spent days and sometimes weeks at Bentham's town house or his country place, Ford Abbey, Devonshire, and poured out a flood of books and pamphlets and articles, mostly in the Edinburgh Review, all filled with ideas derived from or suggested by or developed in conflict with the head of the group,— "the Master" as they called him. Bentham and Place read the "Federalist" together; Bentham and Hume read and discussed the "Wealth of Nations." Young John Stuart Mill with his father and mother, visiting Bentham, studied algebra, logic, philosophy, Latin, and Greek at eight years old. In these long visits to Ford Abbey, the Mills, Francis Place and some others all read and wrote and worked and quarreled with amiable informality.

The influence of the "Benthamites" or "Utilitarians" or "Philosophic Radicals," as they came to be called, spread and strengthened. Their philosophy was antagonistic to most of the established institutions of the time. It was provocative. It was essentially an appeal from tradition, from religion, from vested rights, from the claims of caste, to utility, to reasonableness. Unless any practice can show that it is reasonable, conducive to the general happiness, useful to society, it should be done away with. No length of existence or respectability of origin or strength of legal claim can justify any custom not to the benefit of humanity at large. Bentham, Mill, Grote, Place, and Brougham therefore favored political reform almost to democracy; they advocated universal education, in the belief that enlightenment alone could enable men to choose what was best; they sought the welfare of the masses; they demanded individual freedom of action for all, convinced that if the individual were set free from all trammels his actions would be for the advantage and happiness of all. Such ideas were spread not only in such pamphlets as the "Table of the Springs of Action," "Defence of Usury," "Rationale of Judicial Evidence," and the "Plan of Parliamentary Reform," but somewhat later were popularized by the clergyman James Martineau, and scattered still more widely by his daughter, Harriet Martineau, in her thirty-four "Tales Illustrating Political Economy and Taxation."

The Clapham group and the Utilitarians were as far apart as the two poles in religion and in many other respects. The latter were anti-religious to the verge of atheism; and held the church and indeed all mystical religion responsible for many of the evils of society—the identification of sin with crime, the severities of the penal code, the sacrosanct character of government, the persistence of many old-world abuses. Yet the devout and the agnostic groups were alike in their interest in reform. The warm sympathy of the one, as will be seen, ran parallel with the sinewy criticism of the other in advocacy of the reform of the penal code, the abolition of the slave trade, the emancipation of the lower classes from their ignorance, the reform of Parliament and many other fundamental changes.

A focus of early reform which would hardly have been looked for was the back room of a certain tailor shop at 16 Charing Cross, London. It was the living room and library of Francis Place, the retired tailor, where he spent most of his time and met his friends and visitors. Place had sprung from the very lowest depths of London, had worked up from apprentice to master tailor and then retired on $5000 a year. He had educated himself, amassed a considerable body of knowledge and the foundations of a library and had formed the nucleus of an influential body of friends by the beginning of the century. He remained for thirty-two years the center of a notable circle of perpetual discussion, and what in modern times would be called radical propaganda. He collected books, pamphlets, government reports, cuttings from newspapers, and kept up a voluminous correspondence of which he retained copies. Some of the ablest men of the time stopped in to chat with him on their way to and from sessions of Parliament, or spent longer periods looking up printed and written material or discussing plans with the shrewd old ex-workingman. Henry Brougham, later Lord Brougham; Robert Owen, the cotton manufacturer and socialist; Grote, the historian and member of Parliament; McCullough, James and John Stuart Mill, the economists; Hume, the radical; Sir Samuel Romilly; William Cobbett; Sir Francis Burdett; J. C. Hobhouse, later Lord Broughton, and others were habitués of Place's conference room. He had, besides, frequent meetings with the leaders of the working-class movement. There was some lapping over with the Benthamites, though not very much, none with the Clapham group, at least personally. The working-class affiliations and sentiments of Place were not shared, at least until long after the beginning of the century, by the Philosophic Radicals, and Wilberforce and his friends generally feared and disliked the working-class leaders. The whole interest of Place, however, was in the practical efforts in which all reformers were interested. Therefore as time went on and popular education, reform of Parliament, repeal of the combination acts, Chartism, successively appeared above the horizon of radical interest, Place served as a mine of information, a running spring of practical proposals, and a constant inciter to action.

His room and its collections were at the same time a reference library, a conference room, a center of correspondence, and sometimes of plotting, and a publishing office. Place himself calls it "a sort of gossiping shop for such persons as were in any way

engaged in public matters having the benefit of
the people for their object." Hundreds of pounds
were collected and spent and thousands of copies
of pamphlets and reprints of speeches sent out. A
certain place on a mantel was the traditional spot
for posting a notice or hanging the material for a
proposed pamphlet. Every visitor who approved of
the project laid what money he cared to subscribe,
usually a sovereign, on the mantel, and Place generally attended to the printing and distribution of
the pamphlet. There is no lack of proof of the interest of the men of the time in the measures they advocated. Among pamphlets thus printed or re-
printed were Mills' "Essay on Government," and
review article on the ballot, McCullough's "Essay
on Wages" of 1826, and Place's work, "The Law
of Libel."

Place because of his origin was in a position to
feel for and represent a lower stratum of the population than either the "Saints" or the Benthamites
knew anything about, and his fiery temperament
made him little short of a revolutionist. He was,
however, so deeply imbued with the individualist
doctrines of the age that he acted more often as a
bridle than as a spur to the actions of the masses.
Yet if the Clapham reformers were moved primarily
by what they felt to be their moral duty, if Bentham and his followers were guided by their philosophical principles, Place and others, so far as
they were influenced by him, were moved primarily
by pure human sympathy.

Neither the Clapham coterie nor the Benthamites nor Place and his friends had any appreciable connection with, or indeed much respect for another body of men who were nevertheless at that time potentially the most important of all reformers. This was the little group of surviving Whig members of Parliament. Their reforming ideas were, in the political sphere at least, the most deeply rooted in the past and the most closely related to the actual life of the present. They had been deeply influenced by the ideas of the French Revolution, and represented that section of their party which had not gone over to conservatism with Burke and Portland. One of their number, in a speech in Parliament, referring to Paine's *Rights of Man,* had said, "I am not a friend to Paine's doctrines, but I am not to be deterred by a name from acknowledging that I consider the rights of man as the foundation of every government, and those who stand against them as conspirators against the people." A speaker who held these opinions had little to learn from Bentham or Place as to the claims of the people for the suffrage. Right through the period of reaction and persecution, before and after war with France had broken out, Fox, until his death in 1807, and Holland, Grenville, Grey, Whitbread, Sheridan, Russell, Horner, Erskine, and others afterward, continued steadily to oppose the overwhelming Tory majority in Parliament and to declare their support, however hopelessly for the time, of parliamentary reform, the grant of religious and civil equality to Catholics and Dissenters, of self-government to Ireland, and of a negotiated peace with France. Although but a little group and politically powerless, they were the nucleus of parliamentary Liberalism. They kept open the channel through which more liberal ideas might later flow. If the more thorough-going reformers found parliamentary methods ready to their hand when public opinion at last supported their demands, it was largely due to this little group of liberal-minded Whigs who had held together and asserted their liberalism through the evil days of reaction.

It has been possible so far to group men of reforming tendencies around either their friendships, their intellectual interests, or their politics, and no doubt still other circles could be distinguished, such as the Gurney family and their Quaker and other connections. But there were at the same time many individuals who either from native temperament or personal interest must be counted as actual or potential reformers, and yet hardly came under any general denomination. John Howard and the prisons, Sir Robert Peel and the bound children, "Humanity Martin," jeered at for his crusade against cruelty to animals, Robert Owen with his model factory village, Thomas Spence and Major Cartwright with their projects for the nationalization of land—all these and many more were genuine reformers, some of them even before the opening of the new century.

Other men were rather critics of existing conditions than proponents of special reforms, but were evidently the stuff from which reformers or sympathizers with reform might be made. They did much to create a reforming spirit. A good example of men of this type was Sir Charles Napier. Born of an aristocratic and military family, but of no great means, he and his two brothers were noted soldiers. His outspoken criticism of government and neglect to cultivate influence made his promotion slow, yet he served in the Peninsular War, of which his brother was the historian, was in sole command of the troops called out when the Chartists were threatening an uprising, and ultimately became commander-in-chief of the British armies in India. His attitude toward social questions may be judged from such aphorisms as this, in his little book on colonization. "As to government, all discontent springs from unjust treatment. Idiots talk of agitators; there is but one in existence and that is injustice. The cure for discontent is to find out where the shoe pinches and ease it. If you hang an agitator and leave the injustice, instead of punishing a villain, you murder a patriot." In the very midst of the disorders he was engaged in putting down, he wrote in his diary "Poor fellows! They only want fair play, and they would then be quiet enough." And again, he declares that the Chartist troubles have been produced "by Tory injustice and Whig imbecility." Writing after reform had already begun, he pays his respects to the particular improvement then in progress as follows. "The doctrine of slowly reforming while men are famishing is of all silly things the most silly,—starving men cannot wait, and that the people of England have been and are ill-treated and ill-governed is my fixed opinion." After attending one of the workingmen's meetings he wrote to a friend that the opinions expressed were "pretty much—don't tell this—very like my own."

Numerous popular writers satirized or criticized or fulminated against existing abuses and thus weakened the support of existing conditions. Adverse criticism existed from an early period but it became more vigorous and more specific as the first half of the century wore on. Such was Carlyle's from 1820 onward, with his complaints of the miserable condition of the people, his "two million industrial soldiers already sitting in Bastilles and five millions pining on potatoes," his thunders against conservatism and conventionality, and his appeals for attention to "the condition of the people question." Ruskin, Dickens, Kingsley, Mrs. Gaskell, Disraeli, came later, in the forties and fifties, when the tide of reform was already in full flow and their writings merely strengthened its force or directed it into special channels.

The reformers and the sympathizers with reform here enumerated were all of the relatively well-to-do, leisured, educated classes, many of them of the aristocracy, members of the ruling class or on the edge of it. They had no personal advantage to obtain from the causes they advocated, they would not gain a penny or obtain any social prestige from the success of their efforts—rather the contrary. They were the typical upper-class reformers of the first half of the century. But it must not be forgotten that there was in existence a great mass of discontent and distress to which reform of some kind meant personal relief from suffering and from what they, even more universally than the upper-class reformers, considered oppression and injustice. Many members of the lower classes at the opening of the century were ignorant, hungry, restless, from time to time riotous, threatening to cut the Gordian knot of their distress by violence. They had their leaders, sometimes from among the working classes themselves, sometimes from that twilight zone of restless spirits hard to classify socially from which so many popular leaders have sprung, occasionally from the upper classes. Shelley's appeal

> Rise like lions after slumber
> In unconquerable number.
> Shake your chains to earth like dew,
> Which in sleep had fallen on you,
> Ye are many—they are few.

was hardly known to the working classes. Yet popular discontent and recurring turbulence were factors of immense influence in the history of the time. To the conservative they were warnings not to allow the lower classes to get an inch for fear they would take an ell, a challenge to keep down the populace with a strong hand; to the liberal they were an appeal for justice, a warning that unless reform was given, it might be taken; to a sympathizer like Napier violence was an intolerable way to reach the desired result, however desirable it might be. If the great proportion of the upper classes were an obstinate right wing, if the reformers who have been enumerated were a progressive center or moderate left, the turbulent element among the lower classes were an extreme left, threatening to fight for their own objects—but hardly to be counted among reformers. In the early years of French revolutionary influence, from 1791 to 1795, in the suffering years just at the opening of the century, and again from 1806 to 1812, in the twenties, and again under Chartism in the thirties, the breaking of machinery, burning of crops, food riots, mass meetings, processions, and popular demands for parliamentary reform kept a muttering and threat of turbulence. But violence, so far as it existed, was sterile; it was not the route by which reforms were actually reached in England. Nor is it the subject of this book, which is the progress of reform by act of Parliament.

All those who have been described as interested in reform, however varied their objects, and however detached their efforts, were really engaged in one general campaign, an attack on the citadel of things as they were. It is not a matter of surprise, therefore, that they all met similar obstacles. Our

next task therefore is to examine into the conditions prevailing at the beginning of the century
that made the path of abolition of abuses and introduction of improvements a long and rugged one.
The first and greatest difficulty was, perhaps always is, ignorance. The instance already given of
Pitt's complete ignorance of the poverty of the
common people does not stand alone among anec-
dotes of that thoroughly English statesman. Clarkson tells that when he described the slave trade to
him he was utterly amazed at Pitt's ignorance not
only of that branch of commerce but of the geogra-
phy, productions, needs, and methods on which it
was based. Yet Pitt was an unusually intelligent
and well informed man.

When Howard described in Parliament the condition of the county jails of England his hearers
were astonished and at first incredulous, though
they were themselves country gentry. Many of
them had been magistrates, and even sheriffs, whose
principal function was to look after the county
jails. They did not know what was under their
own eyes. When Sir Robert Peel in 1802 brought
up the matter of the apprentice children in the new
cotton factories, he confessed that he had not until
lately known about them even in his own mills, and
ignorance of conditions in the factories and mines
withstood the disclosures of successive investigations and reports of inspectors through more than
a generation. The statement in the House of Commons by the Society of the Friends of the People

in 1793 that out of the whole 513 members, 300 owed their appointment to only 162 electors, astonishing and almost incredible as it was to those who listened to it, has never yet been controverted. The fact is that men know very little about what goes on around them. Each man's circle of knowledge is small. The proverbial statement that "one half the world does not know how the other half lives" is weak. No appreciable proportion of the world knows how any other portion lives. The first difficulty in initiating any reform is to induce people to listen long enough to learn the principal facts of the case. The complacent ignorance of facts so often displayed by opponents of change goes far to excuse or at least to explain the traditional bad manners of its advocates.

Another common obstacle was, naturally, self-interest. The first movement in the direction of change regularly touches some vested interest. When it was proposed to abolish the slave trade, Liverpool and Bristol immediately saw their prosperity threatened, and the West Indian planters rose in defense of their endangered labor supply. It was natural that borough owners should resent being deprived of property for which they had spent large sums. For the site of Westbury, which had the privilege of returning two members to Parliament, £10,000 had been paid; £6000 had been paid for one borough seat, £5000 for another. Reform of Parliament meant to the borough owners the loss of these values. Factory owners resisted the legislative restriction of the age and hours of their workers; landowners opposed the removal of the duties that kept up the price of grain and gave them high rents. It is true that this kind of resistance could be overcome. Self-interest was not so insurmountable a difficulty as might at first sight appear, nor did it as a matter of fact prove in the long run so serious an obstacle as some others. In a society of varied interests, such as that of England, no one person or class could permanently prevent action being taken by those who did not feel that particular pinch. And among those pecuniarily interested there were always some who from difference of opinion as to what was their true interest, or from good feeling, or party allegiance, broke the solidarity of opposition. Nevertheless the opposition of these materially interested made many a struggle long that might otherwise have been a short one.

Almost insuperable conservative influences were found by the early reformers in the established church and in the judiciary. The bishops in the House of Lords fought as an almost solid phalanx against any reform of the game laws, the penal laws, Catholic emancipation, abolition of the slave trade, and even such humanitarian legislation as protection of the chimney sweeps. They voted twenty-one to two against the first parliamentary reform bill. The great body of the rural clergy could be counted on to use what influence they possessed in opposition to any change in the customs of the country, good or bad. It was perhaps not unnatural that an established and endowed church, in close connection with the state, its clergy enjoying many privileges, the supporters of religious tradition and the embodiment of moral authority, should be an institution as insusceptible to change as could be imagined. Certainly at the beginning of the century the Anglican clergy were the most conservative element in a stereotyped system.

The higher courts and their judges were scarcely less so. Lord Eldon, Lord Ellenborough and Lord Lyndhurst, the three chief justices during the first decade of the century, in the House of Lords as well as on the bench, in both legislative and judicial capacities opposed changes in the penal code and refused any action looking toward the reform of the courts. This attitude also was natural. The courts enforce the law as it is, not as it should be. The large part played by precedent in English common law keeps the eyes of judges and practitioners on the past rather than on the future. It would be hard to find in the whole history of the courts any judicial decision that has carried human liberty further forward, removed any old abuse, or been conducive to social progress. It is true that Chief Justice Mansfield in 1772 by declaring the negro Somerset free had established the rule that there can be no slavery in England; but he made the decision reluctantly, accepted grudgingly the reasoning suggested to him and his decision was at best but an echo of the cry of the London mob, "no property in men." The most that could be expected of the courts was the protection of individual rights under the law, neither an improvement of the law nor general enlightenment. Certainly no bishop or judge was to be found among the prominent reformers of the early nineteenth century, and there are abundant instances of resistance to reform on the part of both the church and the courts.

Back of much of the early opposition to reform was plain fear. Employers were afraid of their workmen, the upper classes were afraid of the lower classes, Protestants were afraid of Catholics, men opposed change for fear it might set free unknown and destructive forces. Such mistrust was for the most part unacknowledged, and by those who felt it unrecognized as such, but it led them nevertheless to instinctive opposition to progressive movements. Proofs of its existence are to be found not so much in explicit statements as in the credulity and the cruelty that are well-known concomitants of fear. In the last decade of the eighteenth century and the first two of the nineteenth the ministry, Parliament and many people of the upper classes lived under a genuine belief that an overthrow of the government was being planned. Measures were taken to nip such an effort in the bud, or, if that proved impracticable, to put it down by force. The press was restrained, *habeas corpus* suspended, coercion laws passed by Parliament, a spy-system instituted, and individuals prosecuted by the crown lawyers. Yet all modern historical scholars agree that the government was taking measures against conspiracies that did not exist, anticipating risings that were never projected. Fear disabled men from discriminating between the real and the unreal.

In the same way casual disorders were punished with a severity explicable only by panic. As late as 1830 and under a Whig ministry a series of riots in the southern counties was followed by special assizes and sentences of a harshness comparable with those of Justice Jeffreys. There had long been suffering and consequent discontent among the agricultural laborers of that region, the crops were poor, wages low, and prices high. The men tried to obtain two shillings six pence a day, which would have amounted to $3.75 a week. There were processions, rioting, burning of hayricks and outhouses. No one was killed or hurt, yet after the turmoil six men and boys were hung for arson and three for rioting. Four hundred and fifty-seven were transported to Australia for their share in the disorders. There are miserable records of the grief and frenzy of a whole countryside, and the next year, naturally, saw not order but renewed turbulence. Such judicial murder and its approval by as liberal a statesman as Lord Melbourne were the results not of reason but of fear.

It would be as unfair as it would be erroneous to attribute all antagonism to change to weak or unworthy causes or to prejudice. Opposition was due, in many cases, to honest and reasonable difference of opinion. "Many men of many minds." Differences of judgment as to what is best will doubtless always occur. Cases where men opposed one or another proposed reform, although they were familiar with the facts, without personal interest, as free from prejudice as frail human nature is likely to be, and not dominated by fear of results are not unfamiliar. Settled difference of opinion must at any time be counted among the obstacles to change to be overcome by the advance party. This was the more natural at this time since the prevailing attitude toward all governmental action was negative. Laissez-faire, the doctrine that government must restrict its activity to the smallest possible measure, especially in the economic and social sphere, permeated all minds. Even the most liberal hoped to reach their ends by leaving men largely alone, though there was room for much dispute as to what exceptions to this general attitude should be made.

Thus ignorance of actual conditions, the self-interest of influential classes, church and state, the conservatism of fear, and honest difference of opinion made a body of opposition that seemed to set at defiance any advocacy of change. No project for any particular or general reform could proceed far on its way without colliding with some one or other of these opposing influences. The spirit of antagonism to change was perhaps at its strongest as the century opened. The hostile reaction to the ideas of the French Revolution had been confirmed in the minds of most influential Englishmen by the course of events in France, and it had been strengthened in practically all by war psychology. Reformers found it necessary at that time to point out specifically that their proposals did not emanate from France. The force of some, perhaps of all forms of opposition diminished as the century progressed. The French Revolution receded into the background, reactionary individuals in high places died and left more broadminded successors, the critical spirit of the century waged war against some of the strongholds of the conservative spirit, reasonable opponents were occasionally convinced. Yet the road of reform in the first half of the nineteenth century remained an uphill and difficult one and the successes the reformers won were won from a hostile world. It must be remembered that those who were controlled by reactionary influence were the ruling classes of the country, the great majority in Parliament, the guardians of the channels of public opinion. The reformers were a small and, to all appearance at least, an ineffective minority.

And yet the fact remains that reform was achieved. The whole transformation of English society from what it was in the early nineteenth to what it is in the early twentieth century belongs to the realm of reality not merely of aspiration. It was the task of the reformers, coercion being excluded from their policy, to persuade enough men to their way of thinking to get the successive measures in which they were interested through Parliament. In this they were in the long run successful, but it was a slow and laborious process. All the general obstacles above enumerated had to be overcome, besides others peculiar to each proposal, and unbounded faith, enthusiasm, labor, and pertinacity on their own part had to be forthcoming.

A study of the processes of persuasion utilized by various advocates of various reforms discloses the fact that a common plan of operations was followed. It is obvious that this plan was not agreed upon, for however clearly we can now see, in looking backward, that the reformers were engaged in a common task, this was all unknown to them; indeed they were frequently unknown to one another, and sometimes not even sympathetic with one another's interests. Nor was any plan deliberately formed. Nevertheless by force of circumstances, by following the lines of least resistance, by adapting the means at hand to the ends to be reached, by overcoming similar obstacles, reformers worked out a sort of common technique of reform. Earliest of all comes the individual reformer, the "agitator," the man so deeply impressed with some abuse needing to be corrected or some good end to be reached that it becomes an obsession with him. It bulks larger than anything else in his thoughts, he sacrifices himself, his means, sometimes his family and friends to the cause. Some such men have been already named and the list might be made a long one. Howard and the prisons, Clarkson and the slave trade, Romilly and penal reform, Bennett and flogging in the army and navy, Ashley and the factory acts, Brougham and popular education, Cobden and the corn laws, Cowper in *The Task*, and a score of others might be named even in the half-century we are discussing. It is not of course true that this individual brought about the reform; but he was the man who kept it before the people, who was chosen by others because of his initiative, devotion, or ability to represent the cause, or who provided motive force, persistency, and leadership in the struggle.

2 The next step was to form an organization. The English people are commonly stated to be non-coöperative. This is only measurably so; their non-coöperation is usually only a measure of their indifference to the matter in hand. When they hold aloof it is because they do not care. Like others they readily combine for practical ends in which they are really interested. There are abundant instances of organization for philanthropic or reforming objects. To begin with a minor if a real cause, as early as 1788 a group of gentlemen was organized to secure better treatment of chimney sweeps, and induced Parliament to pass an act providing that a sweep be washed of his soot and dirt at least once a week, sent to church and treated in other respects with "as much humanity and care as the nature of the employment of a chimney sweeper will admit of." When the evils of the slave trade impressed not only Clarkson but a whole group of Quakers and Evangelicals, there was formed in 1787 the influential "Society" or "Committee for the Abolition of the Slave Trade." When their first object had been

attained they were reorganized in 1823 as the "Anti-Slavery Society." The spirit of the French Revolution, as it drifted across into England not only revivified old political organizations but led to the formation of the "London Corresponding Society" in 1791, and the "Friends of the People" in 1792, both devoted to the reform of Parliament. This was a perennial custom. A list of the dates of foundation of some typical reforming or philanthropic societies will show how common was the practice in the first half of the century, and some instances may be added from later times to indicate its continuance.

1796 Society for Bettering the Condition of the Poor
1802 Society for the Suppression of Vice
1803 British and Foreign Bible Society
1804 Society to Improve the Condition of Climbing Boys
1810 Royal Lancastrian Society
1812 Society for the Improvement of Prison Discipline
1812 The Hampden Clubs
1813 Society for the Diffusion of Useful Knowledge
1824 Society for the Prevention of Cruelty to Animals
1835 Labourers' Friend Society
1838 Anti-Corn Law League
1839 Health of Towns Association

1841 Association for Improving the Dwellings of the Industrial Classes

1850 Society for Promoting Workingmen's Associations

Factory Act Reform Association

1865 Commons Preservation Society

Civil Service Reform Association

1870 Land Tenure Reform Association

1885 Allotments and Small Holdings Association

1892 Anti-Sweating League

It should be observed that these were not organizations for self-help, such as coöperative societies, savings banks, mutual insurance societies or trade unions, nor for sociability or amusement, such as athletic or similar clubs, nor political organizations; but true propagandist societies, engaged in awakening public interest in some humanitarian project in which they were interested, giving it the united support of influential persons and organized for greater strength.

So organized, collecting funds, holding meetings, issuing pamphlets and periodicals, gathering and publishing information, keeping up correspondence, utilizing the services of members gifted as speakers or writers or possessing social or political influence, the objects of the society obtained a degree of public attention and interest that would have been quite impossible to an individual advocate, no matter how devoted.

The ultimate object of such propaganda in popularly governed England was to get the matter before Parliament and, if possible, secure favorable action upon it. Parliament was the general clearing house of ideas and schemes. Numberless bills on all sorts of subjects were introduced, sometimes with but little preparation, sometimes after some such long appeal to the public as just described. Pitt introduced a bill for parliamentary reform in 1782, Wilberforce one for abolition of the slave trade in 1787, bills were introduced in 1802 for the prohibition of bull-baiting and for protecting children in the factories, in 1809 for preventing cruelty to animals, in 1814 for private mad-houses, in 1816 to inquire into the education of the lower classes in London, in 1817 to regulate the work of chimney sweepers. Almost every year saw the introduction of one or more humanitarian reform bills.

It is obvious that the introduction of a bill into Parliament was by no means equivalent to its passage. On the contrary, years might intervene before success was attained. The first bill for parliamentary reform, as just stated, was introduced in 1782, the first statute actually adopted was in 1832, fifty years later. The first bill for the abolition of the slave trade was introduced in 1787, the act for its abolition was passed in 1807, twenty years afterward. Romilly's first bill for an alleviation of the penal code was in 1808, the Penal Law Reform Act was passed in 1823, fifteen years later.

Getting a bill before Parliament was nevertheless the regular third step in securing a reform.

If its entry upon a parliamentary career was the third step, its emergence into actual law might be considered a fourth. The course of events was apt to be something like this. The first time the bill was introduced it was contumeliously rejected. The matter was new, objectionable, not to be considered; after a second or third similar experience its authors might succeed in having a committee appointed to investigate the question. Ultimately after the taking of much testimony, successive partial reports and the passage of considerable time, a final report with favorable recommendations was made by the committee and the House was faced with a bill. If it were at all a strong measure and lacked the vigorous support of the ministry it was probably again rejected. But eventually, after repeated introductions and long efforts, it might be that the House of Commons passed it and it went to the House of Lords. Normally and usually the House of Lords rejected it. They considered themselves the protectors of the nation against innovation. The long course of opposition of the House of Lords to the liberal proposals of the House of Commons that resulted in their loss of power in the twentieth century had already begun early in the nineteenth, indeed in the eighteenth. The first victory for the abolition of the slave trade was gained in the House of Commons in 1792, but was lost in the House of Lords. In 1818 the House of Commons passed a bill limiting the work of children in factories to eleven hours; it was rejected by the House of Lords. Jews would have been admitted to Parliament when the Test Act was repealed by the House of Commons in 1828, except that an amendment excluding them was carried in the House of Lords. Between 1833 and 1853 six bills providing for the admission of Jews to Parliament were passed by the House of Commons and successively defeated by the House of Lords. In 1834 a bill for the admission of Roman Catholics to all degrees in the universities except that of divinity was passed in the House of Commons and rejected in the House of Lords. In the same year two bills for the punishment of corruption at elections and one for the settlement of Irish titles suffered the same fate. In the next year a bill allowing persons accused of felony to be defended by counsel was passed twice by the House of Commons but defeated each time by the House of Lords.

So a catalogue of almost indefinite length might be made. But the House of Commons was now pledged and at some favorable time, when that House was in a position to bring some special pressure to bear on the other, the House of Lords yielded and the proposal became law. So ended the fourth step of the series. Even yet however, Parliament is not through with it. In the light of experience or in the view of the executive the law needs amendment. Administrators of the law have played a large part in England in pressing for its extension. Ultimately, after ten or twenty or perhaps forty years' experience, all early legislation in the field is superseded by a consolidating act or a general law. So what was at first an insignificant proposal made by some individual or small group of individuals becomes, first, the object of earnest effort on the part of an association or group, then the basis of a bill in Parliament, then of continued legislation, and finally by its adoption in the form of a code becomes part of the general framework of society, as unnoticed as it was at the beginning, but now because it is so familiar. Some form of injustice has disappeared from the world or some kind of suffering has been alleviated, or some opportunity for general well-being and happiness has been created.

As a score or more such movements are studied it becomes evident that their advocates have followed with striking uniformity this general method of overcoming the obstacles which were so nearly the same for all of them. Not every stage has always been gone through with, not every step is clear. Yet what was said at the beginning of this work is true, that the history of reform has been a natural evolution, an undesigned conformity of individuals to the working out of a general development. Without prearranged plan, it may be repeated, an individual advocate or small group of convinced souls has proposed some reform; next an organization for extending public interest has been formed, funds have been subscribed, pamphlets issued, meetings called, appeals made through speeches, sermons, books and newspapers, and the election of sympathetic members of parliament has been secured. Next has come the introduction of the proposal into parliament, and after much debate, investigation, and struggle, success has been attained in the more representative and liberal house. Then, backed by outside opinion, the House of Commons coerces the House of Lords and the measure becomes law. After much supplementary legislation and adaptation to the needs of the country the reform is accepted as part of the system of society into which the next generation is born.

It is a striking fact that no considerable reforming movement was initiated in England in the nineteenth century that was not sooner or later carried to success. It is equally impressive that in the whole course of English reforming legislation there has been practically no instance of reversal of principle or repeal of a law, except for purposes of its extension. As a method of securing reform, legislation secured in this way stands midway between the weakness of mere persuasion to individual right action and the violence of revolution. It is an appeal to the strong arm of the law, but it is a reasoned appeal. It has sought the embodiment of increased enlightenment and good feeling in specific law governing one field after another. It is a method in which England has excelled, and it is perhaps her greatest strength.

# THE EARLY REFORMERS

So far reforms have been discussed somewhat in the abstract, or at least reform has been treated as a general movement. It will be the object of the next chapter to describe some of those important reforms of the first half of the century, as they were actually carried into law; to point out the fact that by the middle of the century the current was running more slowly, and to discuss the reasons for this. It will be a still later task to describe the rejuvenation of reform and its changed foundations in the latter half of the century.

# III

## REFORM BY LIBERATION,
### 1807–1860

THE beginnings of the English reforming movements referred to in this book are now so remote—more than a century in the past—and reform has been so much discussed, here and elsewhere, as a general and continuing process, that it may be forgotten that it was at the time no abstract matter or mere expression of opinion. Each reform was a separate struggle, with its advocates and individual and class opponents, its arguments for and against, its position in party history, its successive advances and reverses and its final victory. It would require a volume to give the detailed history of each, but four important reform movements may be taken as typical and described, at least in outline. A rapid study of the abolition of the slave trade and subsequently of slavery, of the reform of the penal code, of the passage of the first parliamentary reform bill, and of the repeal of the corn laws, can hardly fail to bring out the main characteristics of the process. Around each of these a violent storm of controversy raged, and each succeeded only after long delay. On the other hand, for three or four generations now there has been universal agreement that each of these was a change of the greatest beneficence. We do not have to decide whether the advocates or opponents were right; that has long been decided in favor of the former; our task is to trace the course of advocacy and opposition.

So many incidents in the abolition of the slave trade have already been mentioned for purposes of illustration that its history might well be omitted or another reform chosen except that it holds a unique position as the first great struggle of its kind, which to a certain degree set the example for all others since. The English slave trade had an old and dark history. It goes back to the exploit of John Hawkins in 1562 when after capturing three hundred negroes in Sierra Leone, "partly by the sword, partly by other means," as he said, he succeeded, in defiance of the colonial restrictions of Spain, in landing and selling them to the Spanish colonists of Hispaniola. A century later the Royal African Company, along with its other lines of trade, was carrying some 3000 slaves yearly to the continent of America and the West Indies. In 1713 by treaty with Spain the English government obtained the "Asiento" or permission to grant to an English company or to individual merchants the monopoly of providing the Spanish colonies with 10,000 to 15,000 African natives a year. To the Spanish, English, and other slave-using colonies English merchants carried increasing numbers until about 1770, just before the American war, the trade reached its maximum of some 50,000 natives taken by English traders yearly from Africa to America. Some statistics from Liverpool have been already given; to these may be added the statement that during the year 1771 there sailed from that port 107 slave ships, which transported 29,250 negroes, an average of about 260 per ship. In the eleven years from 1783 to 1793, 878 round trips were made by Liverpool ships, carrying 203,737 slaves to the West Indies. These were sold for something over £15,000,000. It may be estimated that the net profits to Liverpool merchants from this trade equalled $1,500,000 a year. The modern wealth of Liverpool was built up largely on the eighteenth century slave trade. In the year 1771, London sent out fifty-eight ships that carried cargoes of 8,136, and Bristol, which evidently used larger vessels, twenty-three ships carrying 8,810. After the American war the number decreased somewhat and by 1790 the average total yearly trade to all slave using countries was about 35,000. These statistics, however incomplete, will not have failed of their purpose if they show how real was the plunder of the black race, how profitable this plunder was to the white.

The capture or purchase every year of these thousands of blacks in Africa, their transport across the broad Atlantic and the hardships of their life after their sale in America, do not belong in the annals of malevolence or perhaps even of crime, but they certainly exhibit a hard-heartedness and a willingness to gain profit from others' sufferings of which white men may still be ashamed. In all the vast sum of misery that has resulted from man's inhumanity to man, that contributed by the African slave trade is no mean part; but the sufferings of its poor victims have no part in this narrative except in as far as they awakened pity and ultimately revolt in sympathetic souls.

The slave trade and slavery, however clearly distinguishable in legislation, were scarcely separable in the thoughts of ordinary men, and the voices of opposition to the practice that were raised from time to time applied indiscriminately to both. George Fox, the early Quaker, bore his testimony against them, the Pennsylvania Yearly Meeting and the London Yearly Meeting of the Quakers threatened to disown members taking part in the trade. It was criticized by Adam Smith as early as 1760 and more severely in the *Wealth of Nations,* in 1776. It was satirized in Pope's *Essay on Man,* grieved over in Cowper's *Task* and condemned in Thompson's *Seasons* and Defoe's *Reformation of Manners.* The pleasing picture of Friday in *Robinson Crusoe* was a contribution to the protests. Johnson described Jamaica, because of its prominence as a slave colony, as "a place of great wealth and dreadful wickedness, a den of tyrants and a dungeon of slaves."

In the decade from 1770 to 1780 interest in the slave trade and objection to it were evidently increasing. John Wesley in his *Thoughts on Slavery,* written in 1774, speaking of the West Indies says

"It were better that all those islands should remain uncultivated forever; yea, it were more desirable that they were altogether sunk in the depths of the sea than that they should be cultivated at so high a price as the violation of justice, mercy and truth; and it would be better that none should labor there, that the work should be left undone than that myriads of innocent men should be murdered, and myriads more dragged into the basest slavery." He appeals to the captain of a slave ship: "immediately quit the horrid trade; at all events be an honest man." Harvard students debated its rightfulness in 1773. Jefferson in his first draft of the Declaration of Independence, among the many derelictions fathered on George III, charges him with "waging cruel war against human nature itself, violating its most sacred rights of life and liberty in the persons of a distant people who never offended him, captivating and carrying them into slavery in another hemisphere or to incur miserable death in their transportation thither." Various southern members of Congress who favored slavery and various northern members who valued the slave trade objected and the clause was stricken out.

Jeremy Bentham, as might have been expected, was bitterly opposed to slavery, especially because of the harsh laws considered necessary to keep the slaves in order. In his *Principles of Penal Law,* he says of these colonial laws "If such a code be necessary these laws are a disgrace and an outrage upon humanity, if not necessary, these laws are a disgrace to the colonists themselves. A lady sends to Burns "an excellent poem on the Slave-Trade." The poet praises it and pays her the compliment of suggesting some improvements in its form. Men as far apart in all other respects as Paine and Paley, the former in an essay especially directed against slavery, the latter in his *Moral Philosophy,* write in its condemnation.

The case of the negro Somerset in 1772 was at once an indication of the rising opposition to slavery and a step in the increase of that opposition. There were many negro slaves in England itself, 15,000, it was asserted at the time, for the most part such as had been brought home from the slave-using colonies, and were used as personal or household attendants. The boy referred to in the following advertisement in the Birmingham Advertiser, November 11, 1771, was probably brought up in one of the colonies, since he could speak English, and was evidently valued for his color. "To be sold by auction, Saturday, the 30th day of November instant, at the house of Mrs. Webb in the city of Litchfield, known by the sign of the Baker's Arms, between the Hours of 3 and 5 in the evening of the said day, a Negro Boy from Africa, supposed to be about 10 or 11 years of age. He is remarkably strait, well-proportioned, speaks tolerably good English, of a mild Disposition, friendly, officious, sound, healthy, fond of Labour and for Colour an excellent fine Black." The slave James Somerset, who had been brought to England from Virginia by his owner, Charles Stewart, escaped from his master but was recaptured, and as punishment sent on shipboard to be taken to Jamaica and sold. A gentleman, Granville Sharp, who had long been interested in the question of slavery and had studied the law on the subject and recently published a book *On the Injustice and Dangerous Tendency of Tolerating Slavery in England,* learned of Somerset's position and applied to the court for a writ of *habeas corpus* against the shipmaster. With some difficulty the case was ultimately brought before Chief Justice Mansfield. It was thoroughly debated by interested and eminent lawyers on both sides in three successive sessions of court. The Chief Justice, though apparently with some reluctance, finally gave his famous decision: men are naturally free; if they are in slavery it must be by statute law; there is no such law on the English statute book, therefore there is no such thing as slavery in England. Somerset and all other so-called servants in slavery in England were therefore free. Six years later a similar decision was given in Scotland in the case of the negro, Joseph Knight. Thus slavery disappeared from Great Britain.

There was evidently widespread disapproval, in the later decades of the eighteenth century, of the slave trade and of slavery, but there was, so far, no single determined opponent or group of opponents. The typical "agitator" had not yet appeared on the scene. The honor of this position belongs properly to Thomas Clarkson. In 1785, while a stu-

dent at Cambridge, he wrote in competition for the
Latin essay prize of the year. The subject, *anne
liceat homines invitos in servitutem dare,* "Whether
men can justly be reduced to servitude," itself indicates the interest in the subject of the Vice Chancellor, Dr. Packard, who had appointed it and had
preached a sermon against slavery the year before.
Clarkson not only won the prize but became obsessed
with the question. He directed his attention specifically to the slave trade, and began immediately
those investigations which extended over a whole
lifetime, which carried him to every English seaport
from which slaving ships went out, to the African
coast and to the continent of Europe, and brought
forth pamphlet after pamphlet, report after report,
memorial after memorial, and finally his history of
his long and ultimately successful campaign.

The time was already ripe for what we have so
often found to be the second stage of agitation,
the formation of a propagandist society. In 1783
Anthony Benezet, a Philadelphia Quaker, long an
outspoken opponent of slavery, arrived in London
on a mission to testify to London Yearly Meeting
against the trade. As a result the meeting presented
a petition to Parliament to abolish the slave trade,
and issued in explanation of their action a pamphlet
of which 12,000 copies were circulated. In 1784
Rev. James Ramsay, a clergyman from St. Kitts, returned to England and published a book about West
Indian slavery, of which he was in a position to
speak from long personal knowledge. The sym-

pathies of Granville Sharp and of more than one of
the Clapham group have already been mentioned.
The interest in the Somerset case had never died
down and other men in the meantime had become
interested. It only remained to draw these together
into an organization. This was done in May 1787.
The "Society for effecting the Abolition of the Slave
Trade," formed at that time, had twelve charter
members, nine of whom were Quakers, two of the
other three being Clarkson and Granville Sharp.
Clarkson was its first President. It was intention-
ally a small society and is often spoken of as the
"Committee." They opened an office at No. 18 Old
Jewry.

As their title indicated, they determined from the
beginning to restrict their activities to the abolition of the slave trade, without interfering with the
institution of slavery itself. Although the beliefs of
most of the members and the logic of the situation
made it difficult always to preserve the distinction,
nevertheless it was on this basis that they carried
on their agitation. They corresponded with the
Philadelphia Society founded by Benjamin Rush,
Pemberton, Franklin, and others in 1775, with the
more recently founded "Pennsylvania Society for
Promoting the Abolition of Slavery, for the Relief
of Free Negroes unlawfully held in Bondage, and
for Improving the Condition of the African Race,"
and with the French society of "Amis des Noirs."
They formed branches through England and Scotland, held meetings, and within their first year had

subscribed about £15,000 and issued six pamphlets, of which 56,000 copies were printed and distributed. Petitions for the regulation or abolition of the slave trade soon began to pour into Parliament, more than a hundred having been presented from various localities and groups in the session of 1787–8. The interest of the king was secured and he agreed to order the Privy Council to investigate the matter. Their report was presented two years later, in April 1789. Meanwhile, the prime minister, Mr. Pitt, a sincere friend of abolition of the trade, but head of a cabinet of divided opinion and therefore unable to bring in a government bill, promised the appointment of a parliamentary committee for the next year. In the meantime a bill was introduced and carried for the partial regulation of the trade, requiring head room of four feet one inch between decks in slaving ships, allowing no more than five negroes to be carried for each ton register of the vessel, restricting the payment of insurance in case of violent deaths of slaves during the "middle passage," for their protection from ill treatment by shipmasters, and making other provisions for carrying on the trade in as humane a manner as might be.

But what the reformers wanted was abolition, not regulation, and what they needed was a leader in Parliament who would devote himself effectively, perhaps exclusively, to that supreme object. William Wilberforce was an ideal advocate for such a cause. Wealthy, influential in society and in the

Tory party, long a member of Parliament, eloquent, with a high sense of duty, and, perhaps above all, a personal friend of Pitt, the prime minister, it is no wonder that the reformers turned to him and urged upon him this charge. They were successful. He was already one of the number of those troubled in their consciences by the slave trade and was moreover desirous of devoting himself to some mission. In his private diary for the year 1787 he wrote, "God Almighty has set before me two great objects, the suppression of the slave trade and the reformation of manners." Whatever success he may have had in his second object, he devoted most of his time for the next two years to serious preparation for the first. He familiarized himself thoroughly with the facts of the trade and with the prevailing arguments for and against it. He succeeded in obtaining a promise of the support of Pitt as an individual though not as head of the ministry. May 12th, 1789, the subject was presented to the House of Commons by Wilberforce in the form of twelve resolutions to be the basis of a bill. His speech required three and a half hours, and by general agreement was clear, informative, and persuasive. Burke declared that "the House, the nation and Europe are under great and serious obligations to the honorable gentleman for having brought forward the subject in a manner the most masterly, impressive and eloquent. The principles were so well laid down and supported with so much force and order that it equalled anything I have ever heard in modern times, and is perhaps not to be surpassed in the remains of Grecian eloquence." But notwithstanding this approximation to classic eloquence, full debate, and the support of Pitt, Burke, and Fox, a resolution was put and carried to postpone the whole matter till the next year. The next year saw no opportunity for its introduction and by 1791, when Wilberforce brought it up for the second time, the opposition had gathered its forces, and the bill was rejected on its first reading by a vote of 163 to 88.

The arguments for abolition, in and out of Parliament, were partly humanitarian, partly economic. Of the former class was testimony that the negroes were either kidnapped or prisoners taken in wars brought about by the knowledge that there was sale for captives. It doomed innocent people to the horrors of the long voyage through tropical seas, crowded in close holds, chained together, often trodden over and neglected, to lifelong labor, the distress of separation of families and the misery of life on West Indian plantations. It was irreligious, wicked, cruel, and shameful, unworthy of a Christian nation. The slave trade was destructive to those who took part in it; it was harsh and barbarous; a larger proportion of sailors lost their lives on the African coast and at sea in slavers than in any other form of sea service. Other arguments were more material in character. The African coast and interior lands were kept in a turmoil; the slave trade destroyed native industries and prevented the growth of trade in native African products, it diverted capital from more useful investments.

In the negative there was of course much denial or minimizing of the degree of inhumanity; the negroes purchased by the traders were already slaves, captives, or criminals, they would in many cases be slaughtered unless they were bought by the European traders; the periodic appearance of slave ships on the coast made the African chiefs less savage and murderous. Another group of arguments played a large part in the defense of the trade. Bringing the negroes to the West Indies or to the American continent brought them into better physical surroundings, put them under civilized protection, and many were converted to Christianity. It was argued, curiously enough, by those who showed little enthusiasm for making things better at home that West Indian slaves were as well off as British sailors, soldiers, farm laborers, and paupers, and therefore it was doing them no ill turn to bring them into this condition. On broader if not deeper grounds it was argued that the nation was already in this trade and could not abandon it without overwhelming loss. Shipping now occupied in this service would be unemployed, the safety of £7,000,-000 invested in West Indian sugar plantations would be endangered if their constant supply of new laborers was cut off. Slavery was inseparable from the slave trade and its injury would impoverish not only the planters and the merchants trading with the West Indies but the bankers who had loaned them money, causing catastrophe at home as well as in the colonies. "The impossibility of doing without slaves in the West Indies will always prevent this traffic being dropped." The slave trade was one of the nurseries of British seamen as well as one of the sources of British wealth and any interference with it would diminish the prosperity of the Empire. If it was abandoned by the English, it would be taken over by other nations. It was supported by religion and had the moral standing of a vested interest.

This was after all the fundamental basis of opposition to interference. The slave trade was a vested interest. As a member of Parliament said in debate, "The property of the West Indians is at stake; and though men may be generous with their own property they should not be so with the property of others." It occupied and gave rich reward to millions of capital, forming the basis of the whole economic and social systems of the West Indies and essential to the continued prosperity of Liverpool, Bristol, and other ports from which vessels engaged in the slave trade were sent out. Against such economic fatalism the eloquence and the moral and humanitarian appeals of advocates of the abolition of the trade beat in vain. Knowledge of the facts, moral fervor, debating power, high-minded appeal, even calm reasoning were all on the side of the reformers; the solid voting power in Parliament was on the other side.

In the long run, however, the effective force for the settlement of the question was to come from outside of Parliament. As always, therefore, in such movements, two threads must be followed, the course of attempted legislation in Parliament and the course of appeal to the people. It was such arguments as have been enumerated above that made the stock material not only for debates in Parliament but for books and pamphlets, sermons, poetry, and public and private discussion. Some one has counted the pamphlets that appeared for and against abolition during this early period, with the following result, 1788, 43 for, 19 against; 1789, 21 for, 9 against; 1790, 9 for, 3 against; 1791, 12 for, 4 against; and 1792, 24 for, 12 against. In the year 1792 there were 499 petitions for abolition sent to Parliament from towns, counties, and mass meetings; there were five petitions against it. This activity of protest was of course largely the work of the Abolition Society and its members. Their expenditure and labors seemed limitless; as a result the subject passed from the few to the many, the English people as a whole became interested in it, and Parliament was subjected to the steady and somewhat unwelcome pressure of public opinion.

In the meantime, the third introduction of the measure, in April 1792, seemed to promise more success. A bill providing for abolition at the end of five years was carried through the House of Commons, but it was defeated by postponement in the

House of Lords. Indeed it was only the certainty of delay and the anticipation of probable defeat in the House of Lords that had given it its initial success. Circumstances were, as a matter of fact, becoming more difficult. In 1791 the San Domingo revolt of the blacks occurred, in which 2000 whites were massacred and 1000 plantation houses burned, the planters impoverished and many of them forced to emigrate. Though this might well have been interpreted as showing the unwisdom of pouring a constant stream of savagery from Africa into the West Indies, as a matter of fact it roused a natural antagonism to any favor to negroes. In 1793 Great Britain entered the Continental war and for many years the abolition of the slave trade, like all reforms, suffered from the reaction of a war period. The influence of Wilberforce as a reformer was diminished by his support of Pitt in his coercive policy regarding all popular agitation. Parliament resented the constant fire of petitions. As the war progressed and British command of the seas increased, her slave traders, like those in other lines of commerce, obtained a monopoly of all markets where their goods were in demand, and as French and Dutch West India islands were conquered and annexed they were able to pour a new flood of slaves into them. The prosperity of the industry therefore increased enormously and the pressure for its protection increased proportionately. Therefore although bills for abolition were introduced in 1793 and in each of the six years following, they were always rejected or postponed. In the succeeding five years no parliamentary efforts were made.

Yet during all this time popular support was growing; the people were being converted to the abolition of the slave trade, and opposition was narrowing more and more to those pecuniarily interested in the trade or in the West Indies. Even these were losing their solidarity. The planters of the older British West Indies, contemplating the prosperity of their rivals in the newly acquired islands, a success based on a plentiful supply of slaves working on a more fertile soil than their own, might doubt the desirability of the continuance of an absolutely unrestricted slave trade. It was a period of backwater in the agitation. The ups and downs of parliamentary action are therefore of less significance. The next bill, for instance, introduced in 1804, was carried in the House of Commons by a vote of 102 to 44 but postponed by the House of Lords, and the next year the bill was defeated even in the Commons, by a vote of 70 to 77. These numbers were so small as to be quite unrepresentative of opinion, and it was obvious to all that opposition was dying out. What was required was only a favorable opportunity and renewed effort on the part of the reformers.

The climax came in 1806. In January of that year, Pitt died, and it was at once recognized that a new ministry of which Fox and Grenville, old advocates of abolition, were members would bring the long continued conflict to a close by treating abolition of the slave trade as a ministerial measure. In fact, restrictions were immediately placed upon slave trading by an Order in Council and by the passage of a bill forbidding registry to any ship newly entering the trade. Fox died before further action could be taken but later in the year Lord Grenville introduced into the House of Lords and Grey into the House of Commons a bill for total abolition. Wilberforce was referred to by every speaker as the protagonist of the reform; he himself spoke later in the debate. The bill was carried by large majorities in both houses, and March 25, 1807, signed by the king. The twenty-year conflict was at an end. No, it was not at an end, for much remained to be done in definition, extension, and enforcement of abolition. This was the work of the next few years. It was carried on by the passage of successive laws increasing the severity of punishment of infraction, by the formation of the "African Institution," the establishment of a patrol of the African coast, the foundation of the colony of Sierra Leone, and efforts to obtain international action in Paris, Madrid, Lisbon, and at Vienna. It was by 1815 a favorite object of popular interest in England. Wellington wrote to Castlereagh, July 1814, after his long absence on the Continent, "I was not aware till I had been some time at home, of the degree of frenzy existing here about the slave trade"; and Castlereagh wrote in August, concerning the effort to induce other countries also to prohibit it, "The nation is bent upon this object. I believe there is hardly a village that has not met and petitioned upon it; both houses of parliament are pledged to press it." Statistics seem to justify this statement. In June and July, 1814, 772 petitions were presented to the House of Commons with nearly a million signatures.

If it be questioned why the long and vigorous opposition to the abolition of the slave trade yielded so suddenly and so easily in 1807, it can only be said that that has been the way of reform. Familiarity has reconciled men to a proposal that at first seemed shocking. All forms of opposition have gradually narrowed down to the one of self-interest, and this has not been strong enough to make effective opposition to a great moral movement; for after all and in the long run the great mass of men are influenced by moral considerations. In this particular case there had been a long, devoted, and skilful campaign by a group of unusually able and influential men; the relative importance of the slave trade to the commerce of the country was declining, and the slave owners themselves became divided in their interest; opposition to the slave trade was becoming world-wide and it seemed only a matter of time till it should be abolished by all nations. After this long time of preparation a sudden change in the ministry, although due primarily to other causes, brought men more favorable to reform to the front and made the passage of the long-delayed measure easy.

## REFORM BY LIBERATION

To complete the story of this, the first great reform of the nineteenth century, it would seem proper to carry it down to its logical fulfilment in the abolition of slavery itself in the British empire in 1833. This must be done briefly. The intervening link between parliamentary interference with the trade and with slavery itself is to be found in the system of registration of slaves in the Islands imposed upon them by the home government. This was in its origin a plan to prevent the defeat of the law against the trade by smuggling; in its outcome it was the first step in a process of parliamentary or ministerial interference that culminated in emancipation. In 1812 the ministry, at the request of old abolitionists, established by Order in Council in the crown colony of Trinidad a registry in which should be inscribed the name, description, and ownership of each slave in the island. No title could afterward be pleaded or ownership transferred except by change of the record in this register. This would effectually prevent the introduction of new slaves from Africa or elsewhere. In 1815 a bill was introduced into Parliament to extend this system to all the slave-holding colonies. This proposal roused much anger in the Islands; it was intrusive, it was unconstitutional, it was calculated to cause restiveness among the slaves. Parliament therefore withheld its hand until the colonial legislatures themselves should introduce a system of registration. In 1819, however, these were superseded by a general registry regulation imposed by Parliament.

This was the first step in actual control from home of the conditions of slavery in the colonies. The second was the issue, from 1823 onward, to the great irritation of the West Indians of successive Orders in Council providing for the amelioration of the treatment of the slaves and for modification of the Island slave codes. This action was forced upon the government by popular reaction to accounts of shocking barbarities practised upon slaves in the Islands by their masters and connived at by the local governments. Sir Samuel Romilly, James Stephen, and other members of the African Institution published reports on the subject and called to the attention of Parliament what they considered gross violations of justice and humanity. Many of these stories were doubtless exaggerated or entirely false, but the residuum were enough to convince great numbers of Englishmen that the complete abolition of slavery was the only cure for its evils. Even the ministry hinted at gradual emancipation, although under West Indies opposition it continually postponed any such drastic action. Feeling in England was exacerbated by what seemed the obstinate refusal of the planters to introduce reforms that had been urged upon them. The whole body of Dissenters was stirred against slavery and the slave holders by the persecution in Demerara of a Methodist missionary named Smith, whose death as a result of court-martial was investigated and severely animadverted upon in Parliament.

This rise of popular feeling in England against

the continuance of slavery in the colonies was reflected in the organization in 1823 of the "Anti-
slavery Society"—which in turn did much to in-
tensify that feeling. It was largely a reorganization
of the old Society for the Abolition of the Slave
Trade, though many of the original members of that
body were dead and new men had come on the scene.

It was still characterized, however, as the older
society had been, by wealth, legal knowledge and
an almost religious fervor. The place of Wilberforce was taken, by his nomination, by Thomas
Fowell Buxton, who had entered Parliament in
1818, was a sturdy, persistent debater, and belonged
to a wealthy and influential Quaker family. The
old campaign was now renewed against slavery
itself instead of merely against the slave trade.
Petitions to Parliament, addresses to the people of
Great Britain, tracts, reprinting of official testimony, correspondence, meetings, speeches, asser-
tions and denials made up an energetic campaign.

Thus by 1830, when reform was again in the air,
English popular feeling was strongly in favor of
action against slavery. An influential organization
had declared for complete emancipation and the
government had become habituated to interference
with slavery in the colonies, notwithstanding the
protests of the colonists. The years between 1830
and 1833 were a period of intensification of all these
influences, culminating in the introduction into Parliament in May 1833 of a government bill for
emancipation. The debate was a long one, but it

concerned itself with details, not with principles. These were already established. By August of that year the bill had been passed by both houses, signed by the king and become law. The terms of the law are familiar and need not be repeated; what is significant is that the emancipation of the 800,000 slaves in the British dominions had now been secured, that it had been done by parliamentary action and under pressure of the humanitarian sentiment of the people. It long stood as the classic example of a fundamental, difficult, and beneficent reform attained by agitation, organization, and act of Parliament. It was of no slight value to England that it was carried through by so high-minded, devoted, well-informed, and patriotic a group of men.

The evils of the slave trade and of slavery lay largely outside of England. A group of somewhat similar abuses existed within her own boundaries. The number of offenses punishable by the death penalty had grown through the sixteenth, seventeenth, and much of the eighteenth century with increasing rapidity, until by 1800 there were in existence some two hundred capital offenses. They were largely the residuum of "crime waves," that had risen and then subsided, leaving on the statute book the laws made to check them. Others were laws of increasing severity passed from time to time in the hope of putting an end to inveterate ill-doing. Many were directed to the punishment of crimes or misdemeanors connected with the increasing wealth of the country. Some of these offenses were absurdly insignificant as objects of the death penalty: picking pockets of articles of ten shillings or more in value, stealing garments from bleaching or drying grounds, netting fish from fishponds, trapping rabbits in rabbit warrens, cutting down trees on a rented place. Some were ranked as grave from a property point of view, such as counterfeiting bank notes, others from a political point of view, such as appearing at night disguised and armed, or giving and taking secret oaths. All these were punishable, if the law took its course, by death. Trials, convictions, and executions under them actually took place. Certain judges were known as "hanging judges" because of the harshness with which they enforced the law; there were waves of severity as there were waves of crime, and there are miserable stories of the hanging of mere boys and girls for offenses of ignorance or bravado, such as in Tennyson's "Rizpah." In 1783 at each of two successive assizes twenty persons were hanged. In 1785 nine persons were hanged at each of the prisons of Lincoln, Gloucester, and Kingston, and it was then only a decade since a woman had been strangled and then burnt at Tyburn.

But the penal code was more severe than common sense or the sense of justice of the time justified. More striking perhaps than the harshness of the law was its irregularity of application. One judge said of it "The law exists indeed in theory, but has been almost abrogated in practice by the astuteness of judges, the humanity of juries and the

93

clemency of the crown." This was too favorable a judgment, but it is nevertheless true that when the crime was a petty one or the offender young or under much temptation sufferers hesitated to prosecute, juries were reluctant to convict, judges postponed sentence and if sentence was actually imposed the culprit was often pardoned. In 1805, of 2783 persons convicted of crime, but 350 were sentenced to death and only sixty-eight executed. There was much pious perjury. A story is told of an old woman who under much stress stole a two-pound note; since theft of as much as forty shillings was punishable by death, the amount of her theft was assessed by the indicting jury at only thirty-nine shillings. There were at one time seventy-three persons, one a child of ten years, lying in Newgate prison under sentence of death, awaiting decision of the Home Secretary whether they should be executed or pardoned. It was a question whether the severity, the uncertainty or the indiscriminateness of the penal code was its most conspicuous feature.

Punishment less than the death penalty was scarcely more merciful. Transportation to the penal colonies in a convict ship was a bad dream of confinement, privation, and danger, with an awakening to almost unendurable brutality at the other end of the voyage. The hulks in harbors, which were the principal alternatives, have left a record of barbarity which needs no repetition. The county and city prisons, notwithstanding the work of Howard and his followers, were inadequate, insanitary and often foul.

An effort to induce Parliament to change this condition of the law became the lifework of Sir Samuel Romilly. He was a London lawyer, a man of learning and fine feeling. He had read Beccaria and was a friend of Bentham. His crusade for the improvement of the penal law is an illustration of Sir Henry Maine's statement: "I do not know a single law reform effected since Bentham's day which cannot be traced to his influence." Romilly, however, had a burning sense of injustice and sympathy with suffering of which Bentham knew little. Bentham's motives were of the intellect, Romilly's of the intellect warmed at one time, depressed at others, by the emotions. It was in one of the last phases that his life later found its tragic close. In 1785 he went as a practitioner with the judges on circuit and in the next year wrote his first work on penal reform. Twenty years later, in 1808, he entered Parliament and immediately introduced a bill reducing the punishment for pocket-picking from death to transportation. This had the good fortune sometimes sustained by enlightened proposals to which opposition has not yet fully developed; after not unfriendly debate and amendment on the motion of the law officers of the crown, it was carried through both houses and became law. It was the last victory for Romilly and his cause for many years.

His three proposals of 1810, for the removal of

the death penalty from three forms of petty theft, were argued against with sufficient vigor to bring about the defeat of two in the House of Commons, the third in the House of Lords. England had lived happily under the old law; why change it? It was really a merciful system, for its severity intimidated people so that they did not commit crime and therefore did not need to be punished. England was a rich country, and capital punishment was needed as the only adequate protection for property. The law might be adjusted to mercy, either by juries which need not indict or by judges who might exercise discretion in punishment. It was unwise to begin change, for no one knew where it would stop. To these and similar arguments Romilly and his supporters had to listen heartsick and to realize that even if a bare majority could be obtained for a partial measure in the Commons, the solid conservatism of the House of Lords would stand firmly against its passage into law. Such was their experience in 1816 and again in 1818. The debates of 1818 were enriched by a new argument provided by the Quaker philanthropist, Mrs. Fry, whose wide and kindly experience in the prisons had convinced her that the deterrent effect of severe punishment was nil. Prisoners while acknowledging their theft declared they were better men than their judges, for they only stole property while the judges by condemning them to be hung took away life. Instead of fearing punishment after death, they considered the heavy penalties inflicted upon them were an expiation for their earthly sins and they would be correspondingly consoled in the life to come.

There was a narrow stream of success in modifying the law. In 1813 the penalty of death was removed from the offense of breaking machinery in mills; in 1814 hanging alone was ordered substituted for hanging, disemboweling, and quartering in the almost obsolete offense of treason; and in the same year, twenty-seven years after it had been prohibited by the constitution of the United States, "corruption of blood," that is to say, hereditary loss of civil rights, was removed from punishment for treason and felony. Some encouragement may have been found in the passage through the House of Commons three successive times of a bill removing the death penalty from stealing from a shop, though each time it was defeated in the House of Lords. On the other hand, in 1815 a bill in a slightly different field, to prohibit flogging in the army and navy, was defeated without a division even in the House of Commons. It is possible that Romilly, before his death in 1818 may have felt that progress had been made in his campaign, for Parliament had been induced to order the collection of statistics of crime and punishment, and there was an evident interest in the subject and readiness for further argument.

This was shown when Sir James Mackintosh, who had been on the bench in India, and was now in Parliament, took up the work where Romilly had left it. He had been interested in introducing reforms into government in India, notwithstanding his judicial position, and was, like Romilly, a disciple of Bentham. He succeeded in obtaining from the House of Commons in 1819 the appointment of a new and liberally constituted committee to investigate the whole matter. The committee made its report the next year recommending sweeping reductions in the severity of the law and establishing a new classification of offenses. The result was the passage of the great penal reform act of 1821, in which only three offenses remained punishable by the death penalty and the basis was laid for a rational penal code. Again agitation had brought familiarity, argument had brought conviction, and after the passage of some years, a far-reaching reform measure had been carried by almost general consent. Even at the last, however, so strong was conservatism, Lord Chancellor Eldon voted against the measure.

The reform of Parliament, the third of our typical reforms, belonged in the political, not in the legal or humanitarian sphere and, as might be anticipated, existing political powers were even more sharply opposed to any change which would lessen their control. The ruling classes could not afford to have the structure of their authority undermined. On the other hand when a member of the House of Commons defined that body as "a group of Englishmen brought together in ways about which the less said the better," there was no answer to be made except to order his temporary imprisonment for disrespect to the House. A detailed statement of the method by which they were selected could only subject the House of Commons to ridicule. As a result of changes in the distribution of population, the decay of some towns and the growth of others, the enclosure of lands and the rise of new industries, in progress through five centuries and all without any corresponding alteration in the franchise or in geographical or class representation, Parliament was about as preposterous a body as could be imagined. It was neither a body of local advisers of the sovereign, a group of estates, or a national assembly; it was the residuum of the political changes of centuries. It was kept alive by its possession of practically all the powers of government and could justify its existence, if at all, only by the way in which it used these powers. It was a powerful body because it ruled the British Empire, not because it was organized with any degree of wisdom or adequacy. The House of Lords was hereditary or appointive by the king with the advice of the ministry. The constitution of the House of Commons was unrepresentative, antiquated and illogical to the verge of absurdity. The number of voters was small, perhaps 100,000, 200,000, or at most 300,000, in a population of more than 8,000,000. Many, probably a majority of these, were controlled in their voting by the ministry of the time, or by persons with overwhelming influence over them. A member chosen by a considerable number of freely acting voters was an exception. Approximately half the

173576

members of the House of Commons were directly appointed to their seats by individual patrons.

The first serious suggestion of a change in this condition was made by the elder Pitt in 1765, the first attempt to pass a parliamentary reform act was by the younger Pitt when he became prime minister, in 1785. Two or three years of struggle showed him that he could not overcome the objection of members to the virtual political suicide involved in any serious reform of parliament, and he gave up his efforts. Soon the French Revolution and the European war supervened, reaction set in, and so far as the ministry and the dominant party in Parliament were concerned, any change in its constitution dropped out of the field of practical politics. It remained after 1792 a part, though an inconspicuous part of the program of the liberal Whigs.

In the country at large, however, reform of Parliament became a part of that almost undifferentiated mass of dissatisfaction, desire for reform and constantly recurring threat of the use of force among the unrepresented classes that marked the later years of the eighteenth and the early years of the nineteenth century. From time to time it emerged as a specific popular demand. The "rotten boroughs" should be disfranchised, Parliament should be elected every year, there should be universal suffrage, and other changes were urged. But it lacked a foothold that would give it entrance upon the road to success. It was only men of unusual vision among the Tories or of especially liberal political traditions among the Whigs who did not dread and oppose any change in the make-up of Parliament. Accordingly such few proposals as were made were overwhelmingly rejected.

The early decades of the century passed till in 1830 parliamentary reform was almost suddenly transformed from a visionary project of a few liberals and radicals and a vague demand of the dissatisfied masses to a matter of practical possibility. This arose from a combination of occurrences. It was necessary, on account of the death of George IV in May 1830, to hold a new election for Parliament. A serious split had developed in recent years in the Tory party, and a popular revolution had broken out in France which heartened liberals all through Europe. The Whigs therefore entered the elections with special vigor and hope of success, and when it proved that a Parliament had been chosen with many new elements and a new spirit, the old question of parliamentary reform was immediately brought forward by the more advanced members of the party. The Duke of Wellington, who was then prime minister and had not been averse to a liberal treatment of the Catholic claims and to some social reforms, could not bring himself to consider any political change, and made in the debate on the king's speech his famous avowal: "He had never read or heard of any measure up to the present moment which could in any degree satisfy his mind that the state of the representation could be improved or be made more satisfactory to the

101

country at large than at the present moment. He
was fully convinced that the country possessed at
the present moment a legislature which answered
all the good purposes of legislation, and this to a
greater degree than any legislature ever had answered in any country whatever."

But the new Parliament was restive and critical
of the ministry, so after a few days of debate,
Wellington resigned, and Lord Grey, the "Lord
Grey of the Reform Bill," a lifelong advocate of
reform of Parliament, became prime minister and
constructed a ministry on that basis. A comparatively thoroughgoing reform bill was drawn up and
introduced by the ministry. Lord John Russell in
his speech of introduction pictured the proverbial
visitor from a distant planet smitten with astonish-
ment at the vagaries and absurdities of the English
representative system, and Wellington reiterated his
argument that all such criticism was insignificant in
view of the excellent performances of the English
government. Ministers read the long list of small
towns whose separate representation they proposed to abolish or decrease and members broke into
incredulous laughter at what they considered the
radicalism of the proposals.

It was obvious that inside of Parliament reform
was looked upon with much hesitation and dislike.
Outside, however, the proposals of the ministry
were hailed with delight. Multitudes who had no
vote and indeed under the new proposals would
have no vote, yet welcomed the break in the old

deadlock, and in support of the ministry raised the cry, "the bill, the whole bill and nothing but the bill." Nevertheless the bill was defeated by the House of Commons. It was perhaps too much to expect enough members to vote in favor of their own removal from prominence and power. It is rather a matter of surprise that so many voted with the ministry, although success of the bill would vacate the seats for which they or their supporters had in many cases paid large sums, and deprive of their patronage those to whom they owed their appointment. It was a hard struggle between the old and the new. But it was already a changed world since the beginning of the century, a world in which reform came constantly more easily.

The ministry, pledged to their bill, dissolved Parliament and, supported by their influence, the new elections justified their action. When the bill, slightly changed, was again introduced in the new Parliament it was passed by the House of Commons, September 1831. But the House of Lords had still to be reckoned with. Notwithstanding that the bill affected the House of Commons alone, the Lords gave it short shrift and defeated it by a large vote in October 1831. The ministry were now at the end of their tether, at least so far as common practice extends, and not being able to carry out their pledge they resigned. The King called the Duke of Wellington to become again prime minister.

Now ensued one of the most serious crises in English history. Revolution was near. A king and an unpopular ministry had just been overthrown in France; if the king and his self-chosen minister set themselves up against the general wish what was to prevent a conflict in England? As soon as the reform of Parliament rose to the surface as a definite possibility the old popular desire for a more representative form of government had reasserted itself as a formal demand. It had been an element in all agitation since 1780; now with the support of one house of Parliament and a prospect of success, organized groups of men drew together in various parts of the country with the old cry. Such was the "Birmingham Political Union for the Protection of Public Rights," under the leadership of Thomas Attwood, a man of unusual organizing power, some wealth and position. Francis Place reorganized the old National Political Unions in London. On their model others were formed and entered into correspondence, forming a loose league for the advocacy of immediate parliamentary reform. Through the early stages of the bill they kept up an outside agitation parallel with the steps of its progress in the House. When the House of Lords defeated it and the Duke of Wellington took office in opposition to Lord Grey the clubs showed a sinister front. Drilling was reported, arms were secreted, a few soldiers deserted, there were reports that General Charles Napier, the last man in the kingdom, as a matter of fact, to condone rebellion, however much he might sympathize with popular sufferings, was to be asked to form and lead a National Guard, as La-

fayette had done in France. "Low political unions,"
as they were called, in contrast with the older and
more moderate unions, were formed under newer
and more reckless leaders. There was some rioting.
In London the windows in the house of the Duke
of Wellington were broken; in Nottingham the town
house of the Duke of Newcastle was burnt; in
Bristol the city hall, the bishop's residence and
some forty other houses were burnt; on the fifth
of November, Guy Fawkes' day, in many places
figures of bishops, most of whom had voted in the
House of Lords against the reform bill, were substituted for the usual "Guy." Even so conservative
an authority as the London Times believed that the
unions would fight if troops were sent to dissolve
them.

But the more moderate lower class leaders such
as Place, Grote, Hobhouse, Attwood and others
busied themselves in urging restraint upon the more
extreme. Place had a plan for substituting financial
for physical violence by displaying in windows cards
with the words "Run on the Bank and stop the
Duke," "To stop the Duke, go for gold," believing
that a sudden withdrawal of funds from the Bank
would cause such a crisis in the affairs of the city
that pressure would be brought to bear by business
men to force the return of Lord Grey to office.

What would have been the outcome of this dangerous crisis if it had continued long cannot be known,
for after a few days the Duke gave up his task of
trying to form a ministry in opposition to the ma-

jority in the House of Commons and advised the king to recall Grey. The price the ministers asked for returning to office was the king's agreement to use his power of creating nobles to appoint enough new peers pledged to the reform bill to change the majority in the House of Lords from an unfavorable to a favorable one. There was ancient and obscure precedent for such action, but it was distasteful even to those who utilized it to secure the victory which by this time seemed indispensable. It is a curious chance that this humiliation of the House of Lords should have been brought about by one of their own number, a representative of the semi-feudal nobility, supported by a ministry, half of whom were members of the old aristocracy, and by a House of Commons so largely their appointees. However, it guaranteed the passage of the reform bill, warded off the danger of serious disorder and changed popular feeling from threats to rejoicing.

It was not even necessary to create the new peers, for when the ministry presented the bill for the third time to the House of Commons, and it was carried for the second time by a still greater majority than before, by common agreement the peers who were still opposed remained away and it passed the House of Lords by a vote of 106 to 27. It was signed, though reluctantly, by the king, and became the Reform Act of 1832, the first of the four parliamentary reform acts which have effected the political progress of Great Britain within a century from aristocracy to democracy.

106

The passage of the Reform Bill of 1832 was one of the most important events in British history. If succeeding acts of political self-sacrifice have been secured from Parliament in 1867, 1884 and 1918; if the history of modern England has, so far, been free from revolution; if those who are bent upon change have usually been willing to await the slow processes of persuasion; if, to return to the thesis of this work, the history of reform in England has been reform by statute, this is largely the result of the precedent set by the reform bill struggle of 1830–1832. Its passage was secured by steady pressure; pressure of Parliament upon the king; pressure of the House of Commons upon the House of Lords; pressure of the electorate upon the House of Commons and, in the last resort, pressure of a crude and poorly organized and inadequately expressed but clearly existent public opinion upon those who could alone transform popular wish into law. The fullest credit and recognition is due to the aristocratic leaders such as Earl Grey and Lord John Russell who were the interpreters and firm protagonists of this inchoate public opinion. For if the people could obtain what they wished by sufficient peaceful pressure on Parliament why should they resort to force? Such was the lesson well learned in 1832.

To discover the evils needing reform and to trace the beginnings of the effort to correct those evils, it has usually been necessary to dig into the somewhat arid decades lying at the close of the eighteenth and

at the opening of the nineteenth century. The repeal
of the corn laws, the remaining reform measure we
have chosen to typify the first half of the century,
comes much later. It is true that the high tariff
placed upon the importation of wheat and other
grains dates from 1815. It was clearly a class provision and it was carried against the bitter protests
of the lower classes and their representatives. It
belongs to the period of reaction. It was intended
to keep the price of wheat as near as might be at
$2.50 a bushel and of other grains in proportion,
for the encouragement of home production of food,
and redounded of course primarily, in a country of
tenant farmers, to the advantage of the land-owning
classes by keeping up rents. Popular opposition
never entirely died down. Ebenezer Elliott's bitter
"Corn Law Rhymes" were published in 1831

> England! What for mine and me,
> What hath bread-tax done for thee?
> It hath shown what kinglings are
> Stripped the hideous idols bare,
> Sold thy greatness, stained thy name,
> Struck thee from the rolls of fame.

The corn laws are constantly mentioned along
with the unrepresentative Parliament, taxes, low
wages, high prices, unemployment, the game laws,
and the new poor law, in the complaints of radicals and other critics of the times.

It was not until 1838, however, that a clear-cut
agitation for their repeal was begun. September
twenty-fourth of that year, seven gentlemen met

at the York Hotel, Manchester, and formed the "Anti-Corn Law Association." They appointed an executive committee and a treasurer, and three months later opened their campaign by issuing a public statement of their objects and appealing for members and subscriptions. Their object was a plain one, to remove the import duties of 1815 on grain. There had been modifications but no serious change in the intervening quarter of a century. The price of the principal food stuffs used by the English people was still much higher than it might be if the tariff were repealed. The founders of the "Association," or the "League" as it soon came to be called, were a group of wealthy men, as the size of the contributions to the cause indicated, and many substantial men soon rallied to its support. At one of the early meetings, which lasted but an hour and a half, £60,000 was subscribed. At the first anniversary dinner six hundred prominent men were present.

. The leaders were mostly manufacturers to whose interests the existing corn laws were obviously opposed, since they both made food high and limited exports. But the arguments used were not in the main class arguments. From full conviction the advocates of repeal pleaded that it would be for the general advantage—lower prices for the necessities of life, larger sales abroad for England's special products, more employment, and a greater increase of wealth for all. On the other hand these arguments had to be used in a Parliament the great majority of which found its apparent or real interest in a retention of the law as it was. A twofold campaign was therefore kept up, as in the other cases described: an effort to convince Parliament and an effort to bring an overwhelming popular pressure to bear on Parliament.

The League was fortunate in its leading orators. Few speakers for a cause have been more vigorous in reasoning and more skilful in persuasion than Richard Cobden, and to these qualities John Bright added an eloquence scarcely surpassed in the century. These powers were used both inside and outside of Parliament. The League trained lecturers, established newspapers, published pamphlets, and held meetings, quite in the way of the old anti-slave trade agitation, with the added wealth, activity, and experience of a later generation.

There was much difficulty in gaining the support of the lower classes, interested as they were in the contemporaneous agitation for the Charter, and the employing manufacturers had naturally to overcome considerable suspicion on the part of their employees. At an early public meeting called by the League, a group of workingmen's leaders present interrupted proceedings and secured the passage of the following opposition resolution: "That it is the opinion of this meeting that though the Corn Law is an injurious tax, yet the present House of Commons will never repeal that law so as to be beneficial to the working classes, and this meeting is of the opinion that the present Corn Law agitation is made up for the purpose of diverting the minds of the people from the only remedy of all political grievances. Therefore it is necessary that the people should first be in possession of their political rights to effect the repeal of the Corn Law." Eventually, however, the movement captured the great body of the workingmen, at least in the manufacturing regions, and in great numbers they attended the meetings, took part in processions, and signed petitions for repeal.

Yet few of these men had votes, and although the little group of free-trade members of Parliament gradually grew in the years from 1840 to 1845, introduced frequent motions and kept up almost continuous debate, the great Conservative majority and the overwhelming agricultural interest of the house seemed impregnable. How long a campaign would have been necessary to secure victory, had not nature herself intervened, is now undiscoverable. In 1845 the potato-blight fell on Ireland and, to a less destructive degree, on England. The principal reliance of the Irish people and a large part of the food of the lower classes in England suddenly failed; a veritable famine ensued. To meet the needs and diminish the sufferings of the people grain had to be imported from foreign countries in far larger amounts than in ordinary years, as contributions or in the regular way of trade, and of course under the law all this had to pay import duties. The unreasonableness of such a system, by which to the necessary cost of relief this vast additional expense

111

had to be added, was obvious. The government had to buy in the open market provisions the cost of which it had largely increased by its own collection of import duties upon them. Prices were artificially kept high just when they should be low. The prime minister, Sir Robert Peel, and some other members of the ministry were already shaken by the continuous pressure of the free-trade argument, and now, to the extreme disapproval of a great part of their party, they used all the prestige of the government to carry through Parliament a virtual repeal of the corn laws. The statute passed in 1846, making the importation of food practically free, has ever since been a fundamental part of English policy.

This is but a brief outline of the history of four emancipation movements, extending through the first half of the nineteenth century. They would in themselves be sufficient to justify the name "Epoch of Reform," often given to this period. The justification would be still clearer if we could give a similar account of the removal of the disabilities of Roman Catholics and Dissenters, of the repeal of the old poor law and the statute of apprentices, of the truck acts, of the long series of factory and mining acts for the relief of children and women workers, of the laws for the prevention of cruelty to children and animals, of the parliamentary grants for elementary education, of the repeal of the navigation acts, and of many other laws enriching the statute book. A partial list of such acts may somewhat serve the purpose.

1802  First factory act

1807  Abolition of the slave trade

1808  Beginning of amelioration of the penal code

1812  Protection of chimney sweeps

1812  Repeal of death penalty for soldiers begging without a pass

1812  Non-conformist relief act

1813  Repeal of act of apprentices

1814  Hanging substituted for disemboweling and quartering for treason

1814  Flogging of adults in alms-houses forbidden

1815  Abolition of jail fees

1816  Abolition of the pillory

1817  Abolition of public whipping of women

1817  Beginning of amelioration of the game laws

1817  First truck act

1819  First factory act for free children

1819  Friendly societies act

1820  Act for reform of the penal code

1820  First education act

1822  Cruelty to animals act

1824  Repeal of the combination acts

1828  Repeal of the test and corporations acts

1829  Roman Catholic relief act

1831  Bill permitting those not landowners to shoot game

1832  First parliamentary reform act

1833  First parliamentary grant for education

1833  First general factory act

1833  Quakers and Moravians allowed to affirm instead of swear

1833 Abolition of slavery

1834 Repeal of the old poor law

1835 Reform of municipal corporations

1835 Repeal of monopoly of East India trade

1835 First marriage act

1836 Removal of stamp duties on newspapers

1842 Act for regulating work of women and children in mines

1844 Children's half-time act

1844 Non-conformist chapel act

1846 Repeal of the corn laws

1847 Ten hours act

This is a noble record. The work of the reformers of the first half of the nineteenth century was well done; much relief from suffering was given, much that was barbarous in the legal system, much that was narrow and intolerant in religion, much that was harsh and injurious to women and children in factories and mines, much that was unnecessarily hard in life was swept away; a beginning was made of loosening the bonds of ignorance. In examining this list, however, incomplete as it is, and in considering the history of the time, it will be observed that the timepiece of reform seems to run more slowly as the middle of the century is approached, and as it is passed further study would indicate that it seems about to stop altogether. Reforms follow one another less rapidly and they are less significant. The wave of reform was evidently subsiding. The abolition of transportation to the penal colonies in 1857 and the removal of Jewish disabilities in 1858 are exceptional. The later forties and the fifties are not rich in reform. Trouble with Ireland, trouble with India, small wars, diplomatic disputes, religious controversy, fill the national annals, but they are almost barren of movements of reform. Palmerston, the most influential minister of the period, was as little interested in reform in his day as Eldon and Liverpool and Wellington were in theirs. It might seem, for a while it does seem, as if the history of nineteenth-century reform was over.

A clue to the reason for this may be found by a somewhat closer examination of the nature of these reforms. It will be observed that they were almost all negative, not positive. They strove to remove abuses, not to introduce constructive practices. They liberated men from disabilities, they did not create for them new opportunities. They were almost all dominated by the spirit of laissez-faire. It was reform by liberation. Its work was done by abolition, repeal, removal. Slavery and the slave trade are abolished, the corn laws are repealed, Catholic disabilities are removed, barbarous punishments are suspended, monopolies are withdrawn. Back of the reforms of the early nineteenth century is a philosophy of pure individualism. Hampering bonds are removed and that is all; recognized abuses are abolished and the work is considered done. The reformers of the early part of the century were usually hostile to constructive movements, to any form of association except for temporary and liberating purposes. They were enthusiastic as long as some abuse was to be removed, some enfranchisement to be accomplished; then their interest ceased. Since soil bearing only such crops must in the nature of things eventually become unproductive, by the middle of the century the work of reform by liberation was approaching completion. There were no more such worlds to conquer. Unless the germs of a more constructive type of reform were in existence, awaiting the fulness of time for their development, as indeed was the case, the story of English reform would end somewhere about 1860. It would be an interesting and amiable record but it would be merely an episode in English social and political history.

It may be observed, again, that all the reforms so far introduced had been the work of the upper classes. They had been given to those who were to benefit from them, not chosen or won by them, except in a purely secondary and indirect way. They were reforms for, not by the people. Slaves were granted their freedom because of the humane feelings of the English upper and middle classes; the penal code was reformed by the kindly sympathy and good reasoning of lawyers and philanthropists; the repeal of the combination acts was due to the sense of fairness of the landowners and more enlightened manufacturers in parliament; the poor law was intended by the rich and pedantic to disci-

pline the poor for their own good. The early reformers did not take counsel ordinarily with the
beneficiaries of their reforms.

It involves no impugning of the motives of the
devoted men who carried through these early reforms, rather the contrary, to recognize that they
were not themselves personally interested in the
improved conditions they were advocating. But it
may be questioned whether men of one class did
then or ever can legislate satisfactorily for men of
another class, in any other sense than by the removal of existing abuses. Have aristocrats, no matter how thoughtful and well intentioned, ever legislated in favor of the great mass of the people? Their
limitation of outlook, as much as their class interest,
restricts their choice of subjects for reform and
narrows the extent to which they are willing to go.
Lord Grey, Lord John Russell, and Lord Durham,
who carried the bill for the reform of Parliament,
had not the least intention of putting England into
the hands of a democracy. Wellington and Peel, who
granted Catholic Emancipation, had no expectation
of weakening the position of the established church.
Cobden and Bright, who with the help of the mill
workers carried the repeal of the corn laws, had
no idea of allowing the workmen to share in the
control of the factories, or, except in the form of
ordinary wages, in the profits from them. No matter how enlightened the autocracy or the aristocracy it cannot enter sufficiently into the interests,
needs, ambitions, and abilities of men far below

them economically and socially to legislate effectively for them. Certainly it was so at this time.

Looked at from the point of view of the material condition of the mass of the people but little seemed to have been accomplished by the reforms thus far described. England was more wealthy than ever, and the population was much greater, but the contrast between its wealth and its poverty, in material respects, seemed, perhaps really was, as great as at the beginning of the century. Indeed "the hungry forties" has come down as the traditional description of the last decade of active reforms of the old type. The novels of Dickens, the lectures of Ruskin, and the essays of Carlyle give no encouragement to the belief that what the last called the "condition of the people question" had been to any degree satisfactorily answered. Much suffering of certain kinds had been removed, but extremely little had been accomplished in lifting the dead weight of the poverty and frequent distress of the mass of the population. There was not much in these early reforms for the ordinary workingman. Slaves, criminals, poachers, untried defendants, soldiers and sailors, factory children, dissenting sects, animals, were all advantaged, and the English as a nation were freed from the responsibility for much injustice; but which of all the reforms of the early nineteenth century did anything of appreciable value for the man making his living, or trying to, in the fields or on shipboard or on the railroads or in the mills or in the mines? Neither the laissez-faire attitude of the time nor the class limitations of the legislators favored constructive legislation for the advantage of the ordinary workingman, that is to say for the great mass of the nation. The strongest and most effective of human instincts and powers, that of association for a common purpose, was disregarded. Men were individually freed, it is true, from many hampering bonds and restrictions, but remained unsupported by common action and unprotected from the harsh forces of a competitive and acquisitive society. It is not a matter of surprise therefore that the "bread and butter problem" for the great part of the English people remained unsolved.

## IV

## THE RISE OF THE WORKING CLASSES,
### 1796–1929

A FRENCH writer remarks, "The English nation is saved by its want of logic." It is natural to expect therefore that among the reforms of the first half of the century, negative and definitive as they prevailingly were, and dominated by laissez-faire, some should be constructive and continuous. The "Health and Morals of Apprentices Act" of 1802 was restricted to a few and simple provisions for the protection of bound children in cotton factories, yet it was the fountainhead of a great river of statutory regulation of the conditions of employment of the great majority of the population. The Gladstone act of 1845, giving the Board of Trade some degree of control of the railroads, was an abandonment of laissez-faire in the field of transportation, leading on eventually to a great body of regulation of the public services. Parliamentary reform could hardly be expected to stop at the arbitrary point at which the act of 1832 left it. Germs of further reform evidently existed in much of the early legislation. Moreover the officials who were entrusted with the administration of these laws became advocates of further reform. Impressed by their practical experience with the inadequacy of existing legislation and the possibility of improvement they urged more constructive measures. Bureaucracy itself was a force for more advanced legislation. New ideals and new motives, as necessarily occurs in a vigorous society, asserted themselves, and demanded social progress, which in many cases could be secured only by law.

But the principal incentive to a new and more advanced series of reforms came from altogether outside the field of early reform and the aristocratic Parliament that enacted it. This was the rise of the ordinary workingman, the self-assertion of the lower classes. This force rejuvenated reform, gave it a new lease of life, a new direction, set it on a long career of progress; it opened the eyes of the upper classes to the needs and desires of the lower; it exercised enough pressure upon them to secure much popular legislation, and ultimately put the mass of the population in a position to direct the course of reform for themselves.

To trace the growth of the influence of the working classes, it is necessary to go back to that welter of dissatisfaction with economic and political conditions, visionary ideas of improvement, and recurring turbulence that characterized the mass of the people at the beginning of the century, and to recognize in it certain constructive forces. The most important of these was the growth of trade unions. Among the craftsmen in towns, millworkers in the new manufacturing villages, miners, agricultural workers, and workmen in transportation on railroads and canals, here and there were centers of organization. Men employed in the same establishment, the same industry or the same place formed a union or utilized a society already formed to improve their working conditions. The earlier unions were usually in the old skilled trades—tailors, printers, hatters, carpenters and other building trades. They grew up most often about social or beneficiary groups, extending their common interests from sociability, drinking, and crude insurance plans to matters of wages, hours, and working conditions, and entering into disputes on these subjects with their employers.

In 1790 Francis Place, then a journeyman leather-breeches maker, joined the "breeches-makers' benefit society for the support of the members who were sick and to bury them when dead," and paid his subscriptions regularly, although he seldom attended at the public house where the meetings were held. Though primarily a benefit society it was also "intended for the purpose of supporting the members in a strike for wages." There were about 250 members, and in 1793 when they had £250 in the treasury and were only making at piece work an average of about $4 a week, they struck for an advance. Their employers organized, and after about ten weeks the men were defeated and a number of them blacklisted. The experience of Place in this conflict, calamitous as it was to his already miserable fortunes, led to requests to him to draw up rules for organizations of carpenters, plumbers, and others. Such groups of workmen habitually met at some tavern. Of this kind was the Friendly Society of Carpenters and Joiners which regularly met at "The Running Horse" in London in 1802. There were in London at this time some twenty "houses of call" for journeymen tailors, each sending a delegate to a central group which negotiated with the employing tailors. At about the same time we hear complaints of a "club of journeymen painters that would not work or let others work." The need for self defense or the desire for advancement was evidently already leading to combination. In what is probably the earliest account book of any trade union, that of the Preston Joiners Society in 1807, it is suggestive of their origin that among the few entries on the first page are, "By ale, 4 glasses, 8 pence," "By Night's Liquor, monthly meeting, 5 shillings, 4 pence." "8 glasses of ale, 1 shilling, 4 pence."

This convivial side was not unconnected with their belief in the fundamental importance of joint action. In the stilted language of the early bodies of rules, "Man was not born for himself alone," "Man is a creature formed for society," "The interest of this society is upon all just occasions to assist and support each other." In fact the formation of unions simply measured the degree of recognition by any group of workmen of the homogeneity of their position and the separation of their inter-

ests from those of their employers. Conditions of the
time were favorable to such combination. The government had withdrawn, by the repeal of the act
of apprentices, from any control of wages, hours,
and working conditions. "Hiring and firing," to use
a modern expression, was entirely free. "Any employee can be discharged at a minute's notice . . .
any employee can leave at a minute's notice," was
the reading of a placard in a northern mill. Workmen were left to the bitter wind of uncontrolled
competition. If they were to have considerate treatment they must seek strength by union, and this
meant combination. "In union there is strength."
Moreover business concerns were now of a size
that precluded more than one employee in a hundred
or a thousand ever rising to be himself an employer.
Once a workingman, always a workingman was
necessarily true of the great majority. The similar-
ity of their position, and this for their lifetime, could
hardly fail to strike the workmen in any establishment or industry. Under these circumstances trade
unions were a natural and inevitable growth as soon
as men were sufficiently intelligent and sufficiently
free to form them.

The growth of unions was, on the other hand, distasteful to employers. They found their men less
docile when united. Demands for higher wages and
similar claims made business success less easy. A
man, naturally, would like to carry on his business
in his own way. Joint refusal of his employees to
work except on their conditions seemed like inter-

ference. The difficulty, in a competitive world, of obtaining capital, of production, of finding a profitable market, was great enough; a united and recalcitrant body of laborers made the difficulty greater.

The sympathies of the ruling classes were all with the employers. The rapid increase of the wealth of England seemed linked with the unhampered freedom of action of her enterprising business men. Judges, clergymen, members of Parliament, the upper and well-to-do classes generally, looked with disapproval on any kind of organization among the lower classes. They discriminated poorly between combination for economic and for political ends. During the later years of the century several laws had been passed limiting the formation of political associations. These culminated in the "Corresponding Societies Act" of 1799, which prohibited the formation of any organization with branches in different localities. Parliament had societies for political agitation in mind, but the same policy might be applied to societies of workingmen.

It was an age of individualism; the economic science of the day looked upon combinations of workmen as efforts to interfere with natural law; and deprecated any restrictions on men's industrial activity even when imposed by themselves. There was besides a prevalent belief that employers were benefactors of their workmen and resistance to them was shameful ingratitude. The general attitude may be expressed in the words of Sir John Sylvester, a London judge, in sentencing to imprisonment in 1810 certain type-setters on the Times who had entered into a combination to obtain higher wages: "Prisoners, you have been convicted of a most wicked conspiracy to injure the most vital interests of those very employers who gave you bread, with intent to impede and injure them in their business; and indeed as far as in you lay to effect their ruin. The frequency of such crimes among men of your class of life and their mischievous and dangerous tendency to ruin the fortunes of those employers which a principle of gratitude and self-interest should induce you to support demand of the law that a severe example should be made of those persons who shall be convicted of such daring and flagitious combinations in defiance of public justice and in violation of public order."

"The law," to which the judge here alluded was the common law, among whose resources was the principle that all combinations in restraint of trade were illegal, and punishable by fine and imprisonment. Under this head trade unions could be brought, and their illegality was early declared. Prosecutions under the common law were from time to time brought against trade unions for almost three-quarters of a century, and undoubtedly acted as a deterrent to their natural growth. But more specific law by this time existed. From 1790 forward many petitions reached Parliament from employing manufacturers and others complaining of the formation of trade unions in their respective industries. Parliament was fully representative both of the upper-class disapproval of such combination and of the admiration for business success already described, so in 1799 and 1800 it enacted laws intended to prevent the formation of unions. These became famous as the "Combination Acts." Under them workmen who should combine to demand from their employers any increase in wages or decrease in hours or changes in any other customary conditions of employment should be punishable by imprisonment for two months, and any such agreed-upon regulations or changes should be null and void. Punishment might be inflicted by any two justices of the peace acting together. A sense of fairness was probably responsible for a further provision of the law prohibiting similar combinations of employers against workmen, but there is no instance on record of this being enforced. There were provisions for compulsory arbitration but these also were never utilized. Thus the century opened with a natural tendency to the grouping of workmen into self-protecting combinations, restrained by both statute and common law and by influential public opinion.

For a quarter of a century trade unions continued to be formed under these anomalous conditions. Connivance of employers, where their interests or sympathies were favorable, neglect of the authorities to enforce the law, disguise as social clubs or "friendly societies" permitted the existence of numerous trade unions though it hampered their natural growth. Such as existed were still small bodies in individual trades in particular localities.

In 1824 came the first step in the process of legalization and of consequent natural growth. The laws against combination were in reality opposed to the dominant laissez-faire ideas of the time, and as the fear by the upper classes of revolution gradually died away conditions became more favorable for emancipation of the trade unions. These conditions were made use of by certain trade-union leaders and their sympathizers, such as Francis Place and the Benthamites, to bring the matter up in Parliament. A committee on the combination laws was appointed in 1824 and by skilful presentation before it of favorable evidence was led to recommend a complete repeal of the old laws against trade unions. This was passed with little attention in 1824. Two results followed immediately: first, a wide extension of the formation of trade unions, and a series of strikes for higher wages; and secondly, an awakening of employers to the recent action of Parliament and an effort to secure the repeal of the law just passed. A year of agitation resulted in a drawn battle by which in 1825 the law of 1824 was repealed and a much less complete legalization was granted. A great step had however been taken. "Collective bargaining" was now legal. A combination of workmen to improve their working condition was not in itself against the law.

128

How far they could go in their activities, how vigorously they could carry on a strike, without meeting the opposition of the law, remained to be tested, and when tested proved to be still very limited. Nevertheless it is from 1825 that the real growth of trade unions is to be dated. Some unions still in existence date their origin in some form from this period, such as the London Shipwrights Association of 1824, the Northumberland and Durham Colliers' Union of 1825, the Friendly Society of Operative House Carpenters and Joiners of 1827, the Operative Stone Mason's Society of 1832.

The chief difficulties of trade unionism for the next quarter century came not from without, from the law, but from within, from their exaggerated hopes and exhausting efforts. The excitement of the struggle to retain the law of 1824, the natural exhilaration of sudden relief from the pressure of the law, the reform-bill excitement of 1830–32, optimism and lack of experience led to the formation of a vast number of unions. These causes, with the belief born of such experience as they had had that so long as a contest involved the men of only one trade the masters could hold out longer than they could, led to the extension of the local union into bodies whose membership was drawn from a large area, to the union of men of several allied trades, and eventually to efforts to mobilize all workingmen into one large union. Instances of these are the Operative Builders' Union of 1832, a federation of unions of carpenters, bricklayers, stonemasons, plasterers, painters, and plumbers. By 1833 this widespread national organization claimed 40,000 members. This movement for federation culminated in the formation in 1834 of the Grand National Consolidated Trades Union, covering all trades, asking for a general contribution from each member of three pence a week, and much under the influence of Robert Owen, and therefore imbued with ultimately socialistic aims. It was said within its first year to have half a million members. At first they sought an eight-hour day and increase of wages. In the hope that the Grand Union would support them many strikes were recklessly entered upon. The stonemasons of Glasgow, the hosiery weavers of Leicester, the Worcester glaziers, the London tailors and many other trades struck, and in other cases men were locked out by their employers as soon as it was known that they had joined the union. Levies were made, a shilling a head, sixpence more a head, one and sixpence, in the effort to win these strikes or to give aid to those who were locked out.

The Grand Union was in no position to provide funds; there was very little wise leadership, there was much internal controversy, and employers generally combined to defeat the strikes and break up the unions. A provocative tone in the demands of the men and arrogant refusals of the employers to negotiate with them were equally unconducive to peaceful settlement of disputes. Failure of the strikes was almost universal, and by the end of the year 1835 the Grand Consolidated Union had disintegrated, and the hundreds of local or individual trade unions had fallen into a condition of extreme depression. At the close of many conflicts the combined employers forced the men before taking them back to sign a statement, known among trade unionists as "The Document," declaring that they were not members of a union and that they would not join or contribute toward the funds of any union. The government also, frightened by the spread of the unions, in 1834 struck at them by the prosecution, under an old law against the giving of oaths, of a group of six Dorsetshire farm laborers, who were convicted, sentenced to seven years transportation, and shipped off immediately to Australia. This revival of old forms of prosecution, and the somewhat indecent haste with which the sentence was carried out, brought sharp protests not only from workingmen but from liberal members of the upper classes. A great procession of protest in London, ineffective as it was, and at a time when the great series of strikes was already breaking down, was nevertheless one of the first visible indications of the uprising of the workingmen that we are describing.

The movement was not restricted to the growth of trade unions; in fact at this period the success of workingmen in the effort to raise their position by economic struggles with their employers seemed to be unattainable. Trade unionists had been everywhere defeated and were in despair. Even when, after a short time of taking breath, new and promising unions were formed and the old idea of a general union was embodied in a National Association of United Trades for the Protection of Labor, centering at Sheffield, it was not successful, few unions joined it, and it gradually declined to the position of a local or mildly propagandist society. The general feeling was expressed by a communication from the Manchester stonemasons, that "experience has taught us that we have had general union enough."

The problem of the workingman might, however, be attacked from another direction, direct political agitation for greater control of Parliament, and therefore of the conditions of their life. Thus arose the movement known as "Chartism." In London there had existed from 1836 a Working Men's Association, formed for the purpose of self improvement, reading, debate, and the encouragement of popular education. It was not a trade union. Its founders were a man named Hetherington—an old disciple of Owen—a bookseller named Cleave, and a cabinetmaker named Lovett, and it had support and advice also from Francis Place. Its members were from the beginning advocates of universal suffrage. In February 1838 this association called a mass meeting at the Crown and Anchor Tavern in the Strand, London, and placed before it a petition to Parliament and a proposed bill providing for universal suffrage, the division of the country into equal electoral districts, a newly elected Parliament every year, voting by ballot, abolition of all property qualification for membership and payment of members of the House of Commons. These were the old war cries of the popular agitation of the period of the French Revolution, revived in the early years of the century, and at each of these periods put down by special legislation and prosecutions. The original petition and its proposals were afterwards drawn up in longer and more formal shape, published, and came to be known as the "New Charter" or the "People's Charter," the name doubtless drawn from the Great Charter of King John.

The agitation soon spread from London to the country generally. Two hundred and fifty branch Working Men's Associations were established in two years, including the old Birmingham Political Union, dormant since the reform bill agitation. In 1838 and 1839 numerous mass meetings, with speeches and torchlight processions, were held everywhere; there were rumors of drilling and the collection of arms, and expressions defiant of the government were used by some of the speakers. As in 1832, the more moderate leaders set themselves against violence, and came to be known as the "moral force Chartists," while the more extreme were called "physical force Chartists." The trade unions were gradually drawn into the movement, sometimes marching as trades to the mass meetings with drums beating and banners at their head, at other times attending rather as men of the same class as the Chartist leaders, hoping something might come of it to improve their still miserable position. 1838 was a period of severe business depression. Unemployed artisans, miners, cotton weavers, and other workmen were attracted by the idea of universal suffrage and a Parliament more responsive to their needs as an alternative to strikes which had so calamitously failed. They attended meetings and signed petitions, but would scarcely themselves have initiated a political movement such as Chartism. The lower ranks of workingmen and those in the trades suffering most by the advance of machinery provided recruits for the "physical force" branch but were of slight value for sustained action.

The main policy of the Chartist leaders was to collect so vast a number of signatures to their petition that when presented to Parliament that body would not dare disregard it. They underrated the self-assurance of Parliament, for when in July 1839 the petition was first presented, with what were asserted to be 1,280,000 signatures, it was brusquely refused consideration. In the meantime they summoned to meet in London early in the same year a Convention, to consist of delegates from each branch association, partly to discuss methods of imposing the petition on Parliament, partly to set an example of what a people's parliament should be. The speeches in this body were extreme and resolutions introduced and debates held were almost revolutionary in character.

By May of 1839, the more moderate leaders had generally withdrawn from the movement and the Convention moved to Birmingham in the heart of the manufacturing districts. Appeals to violence now became so marked that the government called out 6000 soldiers and put them under the charge of General Sir Charles Napier, who has been referred to before as a sympathizer with the workingmen but one who would condone no violence. The Convention issued from Birmingham a set of questions to be discussed at meetings through the country which if answered affirmatively would bring about an appeal to arms, and in the meantime would commit the trade unions and all other workingmen to a general strike. It was obvious the movement was getting out of hand. The government was faced with the alternative of permitting the agitation to proceed still further or of suppressing it. They chose the latter and proceeded to arrest a number of the leaders and to dissolve by force the Convention at Birmingham. Deprived of leadership, not ready for rebellion, and weakened by internal dissensions, the supporters of the Charter fell back on their former policy, accepted the dissolution of the Convention, and in 1842 presented to Parliament for a second time the petition for the adoption of the Charter, signed, as they claimed, by 3,315,732 persons. Again Parliament rejected it, and a long, hopeless, and turbulent strike in its support was the only protest the workmen were in a position to make. A momentary revival in 1848, under the influence of the continental revolutions of that year, led to the calling of another Convention, the drawing up of another petition, some rioting, and a still more definite rejection by Parliament. The whole movement then disintegrated.

A full generation later attempts by the working classes to strengthen their position by political means had better success, but so far as the first half of the century goes, this means had failed as completely as the great strikes; perhaps more completely, for the trade unions never actually disappeared. Perhaps the most permanent contribution of the Chartist movement to the rise of the working class was the development of a certain amount of class feeling. All through the speeches and other expressions of the time runs an appeal to class feeling, class hopes and class interests. For good or ill the sense of solidarity of the working class was now a permanent if hardly yet a powerful element in English social life.

In the meantime another movement had been gathering headway which, although always on the verge of the working-class movement has had a quite independent growth. This is coöperation in its modern form. In 1844 a small group of weavers in the manufacturing town of Rochdale, imbued with many of the ideas of Owen, formed an association called the "Rochdale Pioneers." They had extensive plans for joint living, manufacturing, and providing for their simple needs by coöperative retail trade. For the carrying on of this trade they invented such wise rules that they attained success, set a widely extending example, forgot their other ambitions, and became the venerable pioneers of the mighty movement of consumers' coöperation in England, Scotland and abroad. The picturesque history of this development cannot be given here, but it is none the less a part of the rise of the common people. It is quite distinct both from the trade-union movement and from the political aspirations of the workingmen, and its success has been as largely in the lower middle class ranks as in the working class. Nevertheless its founders and administrators have been drawn from the mass of the people, many of its members are trade unionists, and it has contributed to the people training and solidity, and given them control of their own funds.

So the first half of the nineteenth century passed away with relative failure of trade unions and of political efforts to improve the position of the workingmen; the only promising movement scarcely yet established. There was a slight increase of prosperity, or at least of activity after the repeal of the corn laws and the succeeding increase in English trade. Close analysis would doubtless disclose progress of individual workingmen in material and educational well-being; the way was undoubtedly far more open than it had been at the beginning of the century for self-help and advancement of a workingman here and there, but so far as a general advance in prosperity and influence of the working class was concerned the middle of the century was a period of discouragement.

It was, however, the darkest hour just before the dawn. Trade unions were on the threshold of a new and to a certain degree a triumphant growth. The next quarter century, the period between 1850 and 1875, saw them firmly established as an accepted and influential part of English social life. The first stage of this new growth of the unions was obtained, however, at some sacrifice of the working-class movement as a whole. Through Chartism and all the earlier movements, as has been seen, for all their incoherence, unwisdom, inefficiency and failure, had run the thread of class feeling, of willingness to make sacrifices for others, of hope to raise the state of all the lower classes. Place and his friends constantly look on the reforms in which they were interested as a class matter, Cobbett is never weary of ironical references to the so-called "swinish multitude" he was trying to sting to combined class action. Chartism started out with an appeal for "social equality for all" to be secured through "political equality for all . . . by a more extensive and effective organization of the working classes." The new strong unions that were now built up knew much less of class progress and much more of the advancement of their own men in their own industries.

Beginning with the Amalgamated Society of Engineers, the Spinners' Union, the Amalgamated Weavers' Association, the Scottish Miners' Association and other bodies organized or reorganized from 1850 onward, a type of union was developed different from any known before. It existed usually in the skilled and better paid trades, it was restricted to one craft or a closely allied group of crafts, it was a national body, it had officers and a council with considerable authority, and most characteristic of all, probably, it collected from its members sufficiently high dues to create an insurance fund from which payments could be made in sickness, for burial expenses, loss of tools, unemployment, and as strike benefits. These funds, based frequently on a shilling a week payments, made the unions conservative, and required the development of detailed rules for the administration and expenditure of the funds. Strikes were of course entered into, and many lost as well as won, but this type of unions showed great recuperative power, and there are but few instances of unions that went out of existence or remained long under a cloud from defeat. Scales of prices for piecework, rates for overtime, rules for apprenticeship, exclusion of non-union men, and other trade-union principles and standards were secured each for its own industry, by negotiation or as a result of successful contests. For a considerable period general action consisted only in contributions made by some unions to others engaged in a contest. The Amalgamated Engineers, for instance, contributed £1000 for three successive weeks to the London building trades engaged in a long strike for the nine-hour day, in 1854, and similar contributions are not infrequent.

To trace trade-union history during this period it would be necessary to follow each industry for itself, for it was rather a parallel growth of a number of industries than a general trade-union movement; but it may be said that within a comparatively few years such trades as the engineers, miners, potters, glassblowers, cotton spinners, compositors, the various building trades, altogether perhaps some thirty or forty industries, were permanently and tolerably well organized, with a total membership of approximately 800,000. There were a number of weekly labor newspapers, devoted to trade-union interests, the morale of the unions was high and their pride in their principles and standards was great. Most of the skilled trades, in which men went through a full apprenticeship, were organized as national unions, with acknowledged powers, considerable funds, centralized governments, and well-trained and able leaders. Some of them retained lawyers to look after their interests and defend their rights, as did large business organizations.

The culmination of this growth, its most severe crisis, and its ultimate success fell in the decade from 1865 to 1875. In this act of the trade-union drama—for the history of the unions, looked at as a whole, has been highly dramatic—there were three scenes, two in Parliament the third in their own rooms. In 1867 the second parliamentary reform bill was carried, an act which enfranchised the workingman, except the agricultural laborer, who was left outside the pale for another generation. In the debates in Parliament on that measure there are constant references to the trade unions, and recognition that the proposed change in the franchise will give the workingman, if he chooses to use it, great power. Mr. Gladstone speaks of the "enormous and silent changes which have been going on among the laboring population," Mr. Lowe warns against giving the workingmen, with their organizations, the vote, because "there is no saying where they will stop in the downward direction of democracy." A deep impression had been made upon the upper classes by processions of the unions dressed in their trade costumes, with appropriate floats, reminiscent of the old gilds. The sympathy of the English working class with the North in the American civil war had been led by the trade unions. A special trade-union congress was called in 1862 at St. James' Hall, to express that sympathy, where the eloquent address of John Bright reflected perhaps an unintended glow upon the unions. When the North proved successful the unions gained prestige. Workingmen's organizations for parliamentary reform had long existed, and now, as in 1832, they played a large part. A workingmen's National Reform League was formed, with affiliations of the trade unions throughout the country, and the meetings held by them in Trafalgar Square, the Midlands, and the North in

1867 provided much of the final impulse which carried through Parliament that astonishing step in England's progress toward democracy.

However slow workingmen may have been to build up a separate political party, they were now in a position at least to make their desires known, if not effective. They could press their interests upon Parliament in a way never before possible; they had votes. Leaders responsive to popular appeal like Gladstone, and old sympathizers like Disraeli, not only listened to the voice of workingmen expressing their wishes, but gained a new realization of the existence and importance of layers of society lower than their own class. Candidates were pestered by questions from trade unions as to their attitude on labor questions, and even after the elections unions lobbied for workingmen's interests. Mr. Gladstone began his administration in 1868, as Lord Grey had in 1832, with the professed object of carrying out long delayed reforms, including several that interested workingmen; and after he had had his turn, Mr. Disraeli in 1874 declared his policy to be one of social reform, as well as support of the empire and the constitution. Reforms for the advantage of the whole body of the people obtained a new significance in the eyes of the ministers and Parliament, which now for the first time, although inadequately, represented the whole body of the people.

The second scene was the legalization of trade unions. The trade unions were up for attention over and over again in Parliament in the fifties and sixties, and there emerged from these investigations and discussions a series of legalizing statutes which put the unions on their modern foundations under the law. It is not to be supposed that the new growth of trade unions after the middle of the century had not awakened opposition. Although some employers willingly accepted them, and there are instances of amicable agreements having been signed year after year for more than half a century, yet many employers were restive under the restrictions imposed upon them by the united power of their combined employes. The belief that a business "belonged" to the man who provided the capital for it and that he should be allowed to do what he would with his own was still universal. The unions were often not only dictatorial in their relations to their employers, but violent and tyrannical, or so it was charged, in their relations with their fellow workmen, especially with those who refused to join the union. This violence naturally came to a head in times of strike, and became a matter of public interest and discussion, much of which threw the blame on the unions. If the picture of Sheffield in *Put Yourself in his Place* is correct, there was good reason for public investigation of the trade unions. Outrageous abuse of non-union men by members of the small unions in the much-separated branches of the metal trades—the saw-grinders' union, the knife-grinders' union and others, in 1865 and 1866, shocked and angered the community, and seemed to justify the employers in their efforts to suppress the unions entirely. The masters in other parts of the country were locking out their men in a similar effort.

The law, or the court which interpreted and often made the law, was still none too well inclined toward trade unions, notwithstanding the legalizing statute of 1825 and the extended provisions of 1859. A decision of the court of Queen's Bench in 1867 in a suit between the boilermakers and an absconding treasurer, stigmatized the union as to a certain extent illegal, though not criminal, and refused to give legal protection to its funds. This put the extensive insurance funds of the unions, which had now risen to a value of more than a million and a quarter dollars, in an insecure position and aroused much bitterness among their officers and members. The more moderate and conservative unions also resented the charges of violence and injustice made indiscriminately against them and the less orderly and respectable bodies. The result of all this was the appointment of a large and carefully selected Royal Commission on Trade Unions which was given extensive powers of investigation and ordered to report to Parliament.

In the meantime, in the year 1867, two acts favorable to workingmen were passed. The first was the Voluntary Conciliation act, providing for local boards of conciliation for friendly adjustment of labor disputes. The other was a new Master and

144

Servant act—which unfortunately remained a dead letter—for the first time putting employer and employee approximately on a legal equality in cases of breach of contract, and for the last time using the old terms "master and servant," suggestive as they were of a period of servile labor long gone by. The next year an act was passed especially for the protection of the funds of trade unions.

The royal commission contained eminent and interested men and the testimony taken before it roused much popular and parliamentary interest. Their report led to the passage in 1871 of two acts, the Trade Union act, and the Criminal Law Amendment act. The first gave the trade unions in their ordinary activities almost complete legalization. They could not be prosecuted as combinations in restraint of trade; they could act as quasi-corporations, with funds which they could protect by legal procedure; they could hold land and buildings for office purposes; they could obtain recognition by reporting their offices, numbers, and funds yearly to the Registrar of Friendly Societies. The second act, from the point of view of the trade unions, largely took back with the left hand what it had given with the right, for it created a group of new crimes and misdemeanors, to which trade unions were supposed to be specially susceptible. In the hands of an unfriendly court this list might be, as it actually was in a strike next year, extended to cover many actions practically inseparable from an ordinary trade dispute. The trade unionists therefore continued to protest against this law and when the Conservatives took office in 1874 exercised such pressure that after another parliamentary investigation the Criminal Law Amendment act was repealed and two new acts were passed which even the union acknowledged freed them from all taint of lawlessness and gave them complete legal opportunity to develop along their natural economic lines. There was not a session during this decade in which Parliament was not engaged more or less with the trade unions, and if partial and amending laws and laws in aid of co-operation and friendly societies are included a full score of provisions favoring the working classes in general and the trade unions in particular were placed upon the statute book.

It remains in the record of this creative decade in the rise of the working classes to notice their internal development. Its greatest factor was the inauguration of the series of annual trade-union congresses. The realization of some degree of unity among all members of the working class had never disappeared, although the middle years of the century had seen it at a low ebb. Common interests even of the independent trade unions had drawn them together from time to time. These occasions became more frequent as time went on. Combined resistance to the imposition of "the document," the formation of trades councils in the larger cities, mutual contributions in times of strike, before referred to, united support of the reform of Parliament, the founding in London of the International Working Men's Association, in its inception only an assertion of sympathy for workmen who were not allowed to organize in continental countries as they were in England, combined support of workmen prosecuted under the conspiracy or master and servant law, and finally the joint interest of all in the labor laws of 1871 to 1875, brought out combined efforts and drew larger and larger bodies of delegates from trade unions together for conference from larger and larger areas.

The Trade Conference of 1864 called by the Glasgow Trade Council to meet in London is the first of a long series. A second was called in 1866 by the Sheffield Trades Council, which was attended by delegates from most of the larger unions, representing probably 200,000 members. In 1864 a still larger number had been represented in a national conference called to consider the recent decision removing legal protection from trade-union funds. The Conference of 1868 called by the Manchester Trades Council to meet in that city was of such a representative character and was followed so regularly afterward that it has since been looked back to as the first of the long series. In 1869 there was a similar gathering at Birmingham, and although no national conference was held in 1870, every year since there has been a National Trade Union Conference, or Congress, as it has come more regularly to be called. The sixth Congress, that of 1874, consisted of delegates of more than a million regularly enrolled. This was about one out of ten of the men and women working for wages or salaries in England and Scotland. Since that time the annual Trades Union Congress, the T.U.C., as it appears in English discussion, has been an extremely influential body. With its week of discussions and resolutions, its executive council and its parliamentary committee, it has brought the united force of the most intelligent, highly paid, and closely organized groups of British working-men to bear on all questions that interest their class. Workingmen, or at least the upper levels of workingmen, were now organized as separate bodies and as an economic class, given the vote and to a large extent accepted as influential bodies, even by those who deprecated their existence and feared their power.

No modern impartial historian, interested only in what actually occurred, without predilection for or against trade unions, can reflect upon this period of struggle, filling the first three-quarters of the century, without realizing that the trade unions had performed a great work. They had subjected to discipline and lifted to self-respect a million or more men for whom the old government and society of England had done absolutely nothing. They had until the very close of this period had no share in government, national or local. They were used by the government to fight its wars and, as far as their means extended, to pay its taxes, but they had had no control over its policy. Their employers had used them, just as they had used their machinery and their raw materials, to create the wealth of England, of which the workingmen enjoyed but a minute part, and over the methods of creation and use of which they had no control. So far as the government and the ruling class were concerned the working class were left largely uneducated, subject to recurrent unemployment and a low standard of competitive wages. With few exceptions, whatever had been done for their well-being had been done by themselves, in their trade unions, their coöperative societies and their friendly societies, and in these alone.

They could now speak for themselves and did so speak in Parliament and outside. Is it any wonder that a new series of social reforms were now set on foot, that the old process was now resumed, but with a difference—all the difference that comes from new incentives and a new outlook on society? It was not merely that the working classes were pressing for reforms in their own interest, but that men of thought and influence had now a different conception of the lower classes. It was not merely those who were specially unfortunate—slaves, prisoners, factory children, paupers, helpless animals—for whom thought was taken; but for the normal mass of the people, for all whose condition could be improved by common action secured through legislation. It was no longer that reforms were granted to some persons by others, but that they were secured for all or for great sections of

the people by the representatives of the people in
Parliament. So after about 1860 a new life is perceptible in the almost dead body of social reform.
Projects are more numerous, bolder, more constructive, more general. Practices are introduced which
are necessarily continuous, and planned to last
longer in time and to include a larger and larger
number of the people.

The working-class movement had evidently, even
by 1875, worked a transformation in the general
relation of classes to one another, but the work went
on. Of its three elements, trade unions, coöperation,
and political influence, the last had made the least
progress. Immediately after workingmen obtained
the vote by the second reform bill, candidates for
Parliament drawn from the working classes and appealing to working-class voters offered themselves.
In 1869 the Labor Representation League was
formed and several candidates were put up. The
first success was in 1872, when Alexander Mac-
Donald and Thomas Burt, both miners, were
elected. In 1880 Henry Broadhurst, of the stonemasons was added to them. The third reform bill,
passed in 1884–5, gave further votes to workingmen, and in 1886 eleven from their class were
elected as members of Parliament. The creation of
county councils, elected by universal suffrage, in
1888, gave a new field of political activity to workingmen.

Each year at the Trade Union Congress resolutions were passed in favor of the election of trade

unionists, but here activity stopped; no funds were provided and no active campaigning was done, except in individual constituencies. There was no effort to draw these workingmen members into a separate party. They acted almost invariably with the Liberals, often secured their election by arrangements with the Liberal party leaders, and in fact formed merely a workingmen's element in the Liberal party. The Parliamentary Committee of the Trade Union Congress deferred regularly to the plans of the Liberal parliamentary managers. On the other hand, Henry Broadhurst, a workingman member, was invited to join the Liberal ministry of 1886. Representation gave an opportunity to express the workingman's point of view, but did not give any real political power. Workingmen's influence in Parliament was quite appreciable, but actual power was nil. As a matter of fact the opinions of the Liberals had progressed so far and those of the older trade unions had remained so backward that there was little difference left. Conservative workingmen relied in the main on action in their union and asked little more of Parliament than the Liberals and even the Conservatives were quite ready to grant.

Between 1880 and 1890, however, three new factors appeared. Socialism as a group of consistent opinion took organized shape and began to spread among workingmen, unemployment brought the unions into prominence, and, thirdly, a series of new trade unions were formed very different from the moderate, closely knit unions in the skilled trades with the select membership, considerable funds, and well-established rules that had characterized trade unionism since the middle of the century. The growth of socialism must be left to a later chapter. It can only be noted here that it was much discussed and was a disturbing and at the same time a vivifying element in the working-class movement. The other two movements must be deserted here.

In 1884 began a serious business depression; unemployment was greater than it had been for years. Processions of workingmen invaded the West End of London. Members of the clubs of Picadilly looked out from their windows on interminable processions of a kind which had previously been seen only in the East End of London or in industrial towns of the Midlands and the North, the hordes of average workingmen. Meetings were held and radical speeches were made in Trafalgar Square. The police broke up gatherings which threatened to become disorderly; there were arrests and rioting, and workingmen and their sympathizers, members of Parliament among them, were arrested. Protests against this action brought the unions again prominently into parliamentary discussion, and from 1889 to 1894, as twenty years earlier, successive committees carried on investigations and made reports. Fourteen printed volumes, with the testimony of some five hundred and eighty witnesses, testify to the patience of the committees and the interest of the community. It is from the period of these discussions that date the establishment of the Labour Department of the Board of Trade and the official Labour Gazette.

The greatest change of the period, however, was that which the Dockers' strike of 1889 represented and did so much to extend. The docks of East London are a wilderness of large and small harbors in which more ships are loaded and unloaded than in any other port of the world. The more careful work of storing cargoes for export is done by trained longshoremen or stevedores, who had long been organized in two strong unions. Most of the unloading, coaling, and miscellaneous work around the docks was, however, done by a mass of casual, untrained, unorganized, irregular, and miserably paid workers who flowed into this region from all over England on the chance of picking up an occasional job. The white-faced, weak-limbed, thin, poorly fed, and shabbily dressed crowds that gather around the dock gates of a morning waiting for a chance of employment when they are opened is one of the most deplorable sights in the world. For some years efforts had been made by some of their own members to organize these men, but with scant success. Early in 1889, however, one or two previously unorganized bodies of common workmen, notably employes of the gas works of London, formed the Gas Workers and General Workers' Union under Will Thorne, long a notable figure in workingmen's activities, and won unexpected victories in a struggle for reduced hours and increased wages. This success heartened up a small Tea-porters and General Labourers Union, under Ben Tillett, and when a dispute in the West India Dock led to a small and obscure strike, the occasion was taken for a general appeal to the dockers and the issue of general demands. These demands were for sixpence—about twelve cents—an hour, no engagement for less than four hours, special rates for overtime, and no subcontracting or piecework.

The movement spread with astonishing rapidity; the stevedores' union struck in sympathy; the cry "Trade unions for all" was raised, and soon ten thousand men were out, reasonably well organized, and work at the docks was at a standstill. Skilled leaders from some of the older unions, especially John Burns and Tom Mann from the Amalgamated Engineers, two of the ablest and most influential men in trade-union ranks, lent their services. For some reason, possibly the appearance of Booth's *Life and Labour of the People of London,* with its appalling picture of East End life, possibly the prominence of recent trade-union discussion, possibly a touch of fear by the upper classes of what might happen if things got worse—whatever the reason, an unwonted degree of sympathy for the strikers was shown by persons quite outside their own class. Speeches made on Tower Hill were listened to with more interest and by a wider audience than those made in Trafalgar Square. Large subscriptions were made from various sources, including the Colonies and America. It may not be too insignificant a point to mention that the writer of this book, then a young instructor in the University of Pennsylvania, at the suggestion of the professor of political economy, joined with him and some of the older students to send a modest contribution and their good wishes for success to the striking dock laborers in London. Subscriptions amounting to more than $150,000 altogether were transmitted by telegraph, apart for local contributions. It was possible to keep up reasonable strike allowances for ten weeks, when Cardinal Manning and Sydney Buxton, a member of Parliament, were accepted by both sides as mediators and gave to the dockers practically all they had asked.

From this contest emerged the Dock, Wharf and Riverside Labourers' Union of London, and similar bodies were formed among dock workers in the ports of Liverpool, Newcastle, Glasgow, and Belfast. But the most important result, or accompaniment, was the organization of a number of unions among common laborers in various industries. A General Railway Workers' Union, a National Agricultural Labourers' Union and others soon added perhaps 200,000 men to the ranks of the old trade unionists. It was not the size, however, but the character of these unions that was most significant. They were of unskilled men, in poorly paid occupations, demanded small dues, and had no insurance features and no treasury accumulations, except such as were intended to finance possible strikes.

One of them declares in a resolution adopted in 1890, "The union shall remain a fighting one, and shall not be encumbered with any sick or accident fund." The secretary of another expresses the sentiment of his union when he reports in 1889, "We have only one benefit attached, and that is strike pay. I do not believe in having sick pay, out-of-work pay and a number of other pays."

This was quite a different conception of trade unionism from that which had been held by the old unions. It had no apprenticeship, no high dues, no insurance features, no invested funds, no union newspaper, no links with the employers and few with the old "aristocratic" unions. Trade unionism had extended downward to a lower stratum of society than it had reached, except momentarily and in a few instances, before. It is no wonder that this "new unionism" was a source of dread to those who had so long controlled the movement, and to the employing classes. It was more radical, more aggressive and harder working. It was continually reaching outward and downward to organize the remainder of the working classes of England, and continually reaching upward to convert the older trade unionists to its views, which were largely socialistic. It became the "left wing" in the annual Trade Union Congress, and produced a new group of leaders who have played a distinctive part in trade-union history. However, the older unions also shared in the increase of numbers characteristic of the time. The ship-building and metal trades

report by 1891 an increase from 100,000 to 150,-
000; the group of building trades increased in four
or five years from 50,000 to almost 100,000; the
National Society of Boot and Shoe Operatives rose
from 12,000 in 1888 to 30,000 in 1891.

The union idea furthermore spread to the "white-
collar" trades. In 1890 the National Union of
Clerks was formed and the next year the Shop
Assistants' Union and the Amalgamated Union of
Coöperative Employes. Trades Councils also spread
from the larger to the smaller cities. By 1900 there
were supposed to be 2,000,000 regular members
of the trade unions.

Increase of numbers did not necessarily increase
economic power, and in the exigencies of business
depressions, in the great international competition
now beginning, although many strikes were won,
many were lost. The employers like the men, were
better organized than they had been and it is easy
to break a strike in a falling market. In 1893 a
twenty-weeks strike of the Lancashire cotton spinners resulted in a compromise, and a serious strike
on the Hull docks resulted unfavorably to the men.
In the same year began the great series of struggles in the coal fields, against fate as much as
against the employers. In 1897 occurred the great
strike of the Amalgamated Society of Engineers,
with its 97,000 members and annual income
amounting to two and a half million dollars, pitted
against the strong Engineering Employers' Federation. It involved 50,000 men, lasted almost a year

and resulted in a temporary defeat of the men. But there was no longer any question of the permanence of the unions. In the purely trade-union field the working classes were thoroughly, practically completely, and permanently organized.

The less conspicuous but, as it proved, more important development that was taking place from 1880 onward was in the political aspirations of the workingman. It was closely connected with the new unionism and with socialism. The democratization of the trade-union movement through the former made it bolder and more willing to look to the government for action. Each year in the Trade Union Congress resolutions were passed calling on the government to adopt an eight-hours bill and to carry out other functions which in earlier times would have been claimed as their own business by the unions. The socialist ideas which were during all this time spreading among workingmen also took on the character of proposals for immediate government action rather than, as earlier, for an ultimate general reorganization of society. This is all tantamount to saying that the working classes were again turning, as in Chartism, to the effort to exercise a more direct control over government in the interest of their class.

The struggle was fought out in the Trade Union Congress. The majority there had long held that unionism and politics were two separate things, but the authority of that belief became less every year. The object of trade-union efforts had long been to increase the number of workingmen in Parliament; now a more ambitious plan was put forward, to organize all the workingmen's representatives into a separate political party. It was impossible for some years to obtain a favorable vote in the Trade Union Congress. In the meantime a dissatisfied but aggressive minority—all new-union men and all socialists—met separately in 1893, and without waiting for general agreement formed the Independent Labor Party, partly to advance socialism, partly with the hope of inducing the more conservative element in the trade unions to enter into politics. It required six more years to accomplish this. The Congress of 1899 ordered a meeting in 1900 of a special Congress to take steps to form a separate party. Out of this the organization arose, which at the first parliamentary election after its full organization, that of 1906, took the name of The Labour Party. James Ramsay MacDonald was elected secretary and was thus pointed out by fate for his great services in later times.

There is no need to follow the history of trade unionism in its political organization further, and no space to trace the history of that side of the rise of the working class which is based on coöperation. The history of trade unionism would include the Taff Vale decision of 1901 and its reversal in the Trade Disputes bill of 1906, the Osborne decision of 1909 and the Trade Union act of 1913, the "general strike" of 1926 and the act intended to prevent its recurrence passed in 1927. These are all evidences of the prominence of the working classes in modern times rather than of the entrance of any new principle. A table of the growth in numbers of the Labour party tells its own story.

| 1900 | 2 | representatives | 62,698 | votes |
|------|-----|---|-----------|-----|
| 1906 | 29 | " | 323,195 | " |
| 1910 Jan. | 40 | " | 505,690 | " |
| 1910 Dec. | 42 | " | 370,802 | " |
| 1918 | 57 | " | 2,244,945 | " |
| 1922 | 142 | " | 4,236,733 | " |
| 1923 | 191 | " | 4,348,379 | " |
| 1924 | 151 | " | 5,487,620 | " |
| 1929 | 287 | " | 8,364,883 | " |

When a Labour ministry came into office in 1924 and again in 1929 the political aspirations of the working class fell short of satisfaction only in the lack of an absolute majority, and therefore of such complete power as any party can have in Parliament. In the meantime the socialistic principles of the party had been fully accepted, and its history merges, from that point of view, in the history of British socialism. The growth of the Labour party has made the policy, the powers, and the future action of the workingmen the most important political question in modern England.

The only relation of the narrative that has been given in this chapter to the subject of the book is the influence exerted by the rise of the working classes on the cause of reform. This influence was already perceptible by the middle of the century, quite measurable by the end of its third quarter and complete in all its essentials by its end. Its history has been one of unceasing pressure on the course of events. The working-class movement has, in the first place, called the attention of Parliament and parliamentary leaders to matters of interest to the mass of the people needing reform but long unrecognized or neglected. Secondly, it has provided the voting and agitating force necessary to carry many such measures through Parliament. Thirdly, it has introduced a more direct and practical approach to the solution of social questions, with less of abstract and academic reasoning, less of laissez-faire inhibition to action. Lastly, it bids fair to take the lead in the immediate future in all movements of reform, with all the powers, responsibilities, and dangers of leadership.

Other influences conducive to reform have of course existed, but it is this above all which gives the clue to the differences of later reform from the reforms of the earlier part of the century. Enough of the history of reform in the later period to exemplify this influence will be given in the next chapter.

## V

## CONSTRUCTIVE REFORMS, 1860–1914

A FAIR instance of reform legislation resulting from pressure by the organized working classes is to be found in the series of Employers' Liability and Workmen's Compensation acts. One of the characteristics of modern industrial life is the toll of death and accident it demands. Accidents have occurred occasionally, indeed frequently, in the ordinary occupations of life in all times, but with the introduction of mechanical devices and artificial power, and with the increased speed and scale of the processes of industry and transportation, losses by accident have become far more numerous. In a careful study of a long series of accidents occurring in England it was found that 87½ per cent arose solely from modern conditions. In the factories, mines, ironworks, and shipyards; on the docks, on trains, and in the railroad yards; on congested streets, in the construction of buildings, everywhere where men are congregated and the busy work of the world is going on, there are tragic falls, explosions, collisions, entanglement in running machinery, bursting of steam boilers, and, in modern times, electric shock, each of which brings death, loss of limb or eyes, permanent or temporary injury to one or more persons.

It seems that manufacturing, commerce, mining, lumbering, agriculture, life itself cannot be carried on without a constant accompaniment of fatal, serious, or slight mishap. In the especially hazardous trades it is possible to work out an average of accidents that will occur almost as certain as the tables of mortality used in life insurance. Each crane or derrick will once in so many operations on the average kill or crush a workman; from each iron or steel bridge about so many workmen will fall or be struck and killed or injured. It is sometimes said that the construction of each story of a high building costs the life of a man; in railroad yards there is about an average number of men crushed or injured each month, just as there is an average number of passengers or tons of freight carried.

Nor does it seem possible to eliminate these risks. Men engaged day after day, week after week, and month after month in work involving hazards, inevitably develop a psychology which makes them careless of these hazards. Mechanical devices often contain in themselves imperfections which no care can recognize. The traditions and practice of hurried, competitive modern production are none too careful of the human factor involved. A large concern states that in the year 1900 forty-three per cent of its employees suffered injuries sufficient to keep them away from work longer than the day of the accident, though within the next ten years by strenuous effort this particular firm was able to reduce this figure to less than twenty per cent a year. It is a common statement that half of the accidents that occur are preventable by proper guards for machinery, rails, and other precautionary devices. The daily newspaper gives instances enough of accidents happening in the general course of industrial life, whether preventable or not, and a moment's consideration of the steady flow of these accidents through the whole year is quite sufficient to convince any thoughtful person of the fact, and even to some degree of the number of these victims of warfare in time of peace.

Early statistics are hard to obtain, and unimpressive at best when they are but figures. In the four years between 1872 and 1876 there were in England 261 explosions of boilers in factories, causing the death of 308 persons and the injury of 535 more. In 1908 in seven principal industries, there were 3,447 fatalities, 296,338 non-fatal injuries. In 1913 there were 3,748 fatal accidents, 476,920 which were not fatal. Thus for recent times the yearly average is between three and four thousand deaths from industrial accidents, between a quarter and a half million lesser injuries. Each of these accidents involves not only suffering but loss, some loss to the employer whose work and plans are disarranged and whose property may be injured, greater loss to the workman whose earning power is temporarily or permanently destroyed, complete loss to his family in case of death. How shall the loss be met? According to the old common law, if negligence on somebody's part is involved, and in the vast number of cases there is some carelessness somewhere, the sufferer from such negligence has a right to obtain damages from the one responsible. Moreover the employer is answerable for the actions of his employees, since one of the most familiar maxims of the law is that the principal is responsible for the actions of his agent. If therefore a watchman on a railroad makes a mistake in his signals the company must pay damages to passengers who lose their lives or are injured in a resulting accident. If a workman in a quarry uses too large a charge and the explosion injures passers-by, or adjacent houses, the owner of the quarry must pay the damages.

This principle would seem to provide means whereby the money loss to an injured employee or his family in accident cases should be reimbursed by his employer. But the common law had been modified in this respect by a decision of 1837, followed as a precedent in later decisions. This was that when a man accepts work he is supposed to know that it entails danger from the carelessness of his fellow employees and to agree to accept that as one of the conditions of the job; therefore when an accident occurs he must not expect damages. This came to be known as the "fellow servant" or "common employment" rule—that although out-siders may get damages, a workman cannot if his loss arises from the negligence of a fellow workman, as it almost invariably does. If he brings suit in such a case the judge rules that he has no case. Such suits were therefore seldom brought and damages for accidents to workmen were seldom obtained.

This seemed to workmen and to many others unjust, and about 1865 an agitation was begun to have workmen put on the same legal footing as other persons. It was sponsored especially by the Miners National Union and the Amalgamated Society of Railway Servants, among whose members accidents were especially numerous. They argued that the condition of the common law was absolutely wrong. Employers in carrying on their business subjected their workmen to conditions the latter could not control. It should be incumbent on employers therefore to furnish buildings, machinery, trained fellow-workmen, and other conditions that would reduce accidents to an absolute minimum. If they did not, or if accidents should still occur, they should compensate injured workmen, who were powerless to prevent these. Bills were introduced into Parliament almost yearly by working-men members after 1872. A parliamentary committee on employer's liability was appointed in 1876, took evidence and made a report, but no further action was taken at the time. The discussions were marked by much bitterness. It was a confused issue; whether the common law should be changed or not, and if so with recognition of various self-help associations and insurance companies, or by merely leaving the disputes to be fought out under fairer conditions. The matter came up yearly in the Trade Union Congress and great pressure was brought by the unions on the government. The first success was obtained in 1880 when under Mr. Gladstone an Employers' Liability act was passed. It removed the defense of common employment in five classes of cases, including practically all those involving accidents on railroads. According to the wording of the law, in all the cases included, the workman is given "the same right of compensation and remedies against the employer as if the workman had not been . . . in the service of the employer."

This seemed a moderate and reasonable change, but it still left actual practice cumbrous and expensive. Each case that came to trial involved court and lawyers' fees and much loss of time and money. Although many cases were settled by compromise, without litigation, for some years between 300 and 400 cases came into court each year. These tended to increase, rising for the period 1898–1906 to 700 a year. The question of contributory negligence on the part of the injured employee was difficult, often impossible to decide, and left the result in many cases unsatisfactory. It was one of the regular functions of the trade unions to help their men in suits for damages. The work-

men were still dissatisfied and there was evident
room for improvement. It was therefore a natural
next step when in 1893 a bill removing the common
employment and contributory negligence defenses
in almost all occupations and in almost all cases was
introduced in the House of Commons and passed
without serious opposition. It was defeated at this
time by the House of Lords but was carried through
both houses in 1897 and became the first Workmen's Compensation act.

An entirely new conception of damages was introduced by this act. No negligence on the part of
the employer or another employee had to be alleged.
It was enough that an accident had occurred and
an injury inflicted. It was obvious that the idea of
compensation for industrial accident as such was
becoming familiar. This was no doubt largely due
to the practice of insurance against industrial accident which had recently been added to life, fire,
marine, and other forms of insurance. At first many
large firms created insurance funds to which their
employees were forced to contribute, at the same
time being required to "contract out" of the law, a
practice allowed, against trade-union protests, by
the courts. The law of 1897 forbade "contracting
out" but employers could without serious difficulty
themselves pay the insurance, at the same time calculating it as part of the costs of production, in
which case it would ultimately fall on the con-
sumer. Under such circumstances why need there
be a lawsuit in each case? Therefore in 1906 a new

168

Workmen's Compensation act was passed, under which payments in case of accident on an established scale and under government administration are paid to all employees, with a few exceptions, most of which have still later been included under the system.

None of these laws prohibited injured workmen from suing for damages, just as any other sufferer might, under the common law, but the number of such cases diminished rapidly. In 1908 only 200 were taken into court and more than half of these were compromised at some stage and withdrawn. Only one case was brought in from the mining industry, one from quarrying, and seven in the railroad industry. There is of course much litigation as to amount of claims and other points of difference, but the main principle that all costs of industrial accident are to be considered part of the costs of production and to be paid for in the first instance by the employer and ultimately by the general community is fully accepted. Thus an old workingman's grievance has been removed, and in the course of legislation on the subject a whole system of compensation for accident, extending through much of the community, has been introduced. In its first stages this was a trade-union movement solely, in its later development it became part, as will be seen, of a general system of social reform.

Another instance of such general social reform is to be found in the legislation for the protection of sailors, and incidentally of passengers, from being sent to sea in unsafe and overcrowded vessels.⎤ About 1870 Samuel Plimsoll, a London coal merchant, more of the type of reformers of the early than of the later part of the century, began an agitation for the safety of seamen. He had published a pamphlet on the coal trade, internal and foreign, and was thus apparently drawn into an interest in the condition of coaling and other English vessels. He became a member of Parliament in 1868, and in 1870 asked permission to introduce a bill on the subject of government oversight of shipping. Mr. Gladstone's first ministry, then in office and well inclined to reform, introduced a bill looking in the same direction. Both were received with the bitter opposition of shipowners and other business men and neither reached a vote. Plimsoll introduced the matter again the next year with the same result. It has been observed before that a regular step in the agitation for some social reform has been the formation of a society for the purpose, and in fact the National Life-Boat Institution already existed as it still does, published a journal *The Life-Boat,* and was in some degree interested in the same objects. It was not, however, valuable for Plimsoll's, agitation. Instead he appealed to the trade unions. Since sailors and engineers were most directly affected, at the Annual Congress they took up his campaign and added to it their protests and urgency. Later Plimsoll became a sort of honorary president of the Sailors' and Firemen's Union.

In the meantime, in 1873, he compiled and issued a book *Our Seamen, an Appeal* in which much along the lines of the illustrations in Clarkson's book on the slave trade and the parliamentary report on children in the coal mines he introduced a "Wreck Chart" of the British Isles for 1871, compiled by the Board of Trade, and showing the location and number of wrecks and other accidents at sea suffered by British vessels during that year. He introduced a mass of statement and testimony, explaining the causes of sea disasters—undermanning, deckloading, want of repair, defective construction, overloading, over-insuring, and other avoidable causes of wreck or accident. Much of his evidence was photographed from original, official documents, and therefore not subject to doubt, other parts were more questionable or at least susceptible to argumentation. The next year he issued a cheap edition of his book which was circulated widely. He showed that for the last ten years there had been on the British coast an average of about 2000 vessels a year totally wrecked or suffering from other disaster. Omitting collisions some 700 vessels a year were sunk, some 700 suffered other casualties.

The number of lives lost in these wrecks had risen in some years to more than a thousand; in 1871 they were 626, the smallest for many years;

for the ten years previous to the publication of the book, they averaged more than 800 a year. Apart from these were the large number of vessels that sailed and were lost yearly between Great Britain and India, the colonies, and foreign countries. Half of those lost on the coast were colliers, but the greater losses of life were in the larger vessels engaged in foreign trade and with more numerous crews; for these losses, unfortunately, statistics are not available.

Statistics however were not the most important part of Plimsoll's work. It was his charges of incompetency, inhumanity, and greed on the part of some shipowners, recklessly disregarding the safety of their men. Vessels known to be unseaworthy to the verge of rottenness, "coffin ships," as they were called, were sometimes sent out and never reached their first port. Among the wrecks of the year 1871 thirty-six were of vessels more than sixty years old; three of them more than a hundred. Wrecks had occurred when the wind was scarcely more than a breeze, and in open sea; vessels which if well built and preserved might have held together went quickly to pieces when they went on the rocks even in fair weather, and left the crew to drown.

It was pointed out that the temptation to owners to send out old and unsafe vessels for one more voyage, on the chance that the weather would be unusually favorable, was almost irresistible; that the interest of the underwriters was small because the subdivision of risks under the Lloyd's system reduced loss to insignificance to any one insurer; that sailors were usually ready to take chances, though more than one case was reported where sailors had mutinied before actually leaving the Thames, the Clyde, or Bristol Channel rather than go to what they considered certain death, and were taken off the ship in irons for punishment. Attention was called to the fact that laws had been passed protecting workmen in mines, factories, workshops, on railroads and in construction work. Why should not the protecting arm of government be extended to those who went down to the sea in ships, perhaps the most dependent on outside help of all classes of workmen?

This book caused a great furore; it was discussed, abused, contradicted, and corroborated, as such attacks on an old and extensive system with many variations always is. It served an excellent purpose, creating great public interest and forcing the government to take action. A bill was introduced in 1876 and subjected to long and acrimonious discussion. It touched one of England's oldest, proudest, and most essential industries. It professedly legislated, not for women and children, but for grown men; it extended the oversight of government into an entirely new sphere. It was, nevertheless, passed by both houses, signed and became the Merchant Shipping Act of 1880. Since that year every English vessel carries on its hull the "Plimsoll Mark" defining its load line; before it leaves port it is subjected to strict examination, and its papers indicate the number of passengers and crew it may carry. Some instances there have of course been of inadequate enforcement of these rules, and the winds and waves, rocks and sands, fire, fog, and collision still, of course, bring death and loss, but on the whole the noble structure of the British merchant marine is now founded on the solid foundation of wise regulation and willing acceptance of the protection and restrictions of the law.

Parallel with the two bodies of reform legislation that have just been described there was in progress a series of provisions of the law, some restrictive, some creative, which did much to affect the most fundamental of all relations, that of a people to the soil. The land legislation of the period 1860 to 1892 was not so closely connected with the rise of the working classes as were workmen's compensation and the protection of seamen: it was rather an outcome of that wider conception of reform characteristic of the second half of the century, which considered reform a means of securing some permanent benefit for the whole community or for some very large portion of it. The minds of the men and women of influence, who were still the "governing classes," however much the meaning of that term may have broadened, had now come to consider any legislation fraught with possibilities of general well-being reform legislation.

Under the old aristocratic system, the land was the ark of the covenant; it could not be touched.

Such legislation as had been enacted had served either to make its control by individual owners more complete or to facilitate its transfer from one owner to another, not to limit its ownership. A vast number of private-enclosure acts had changed intermingled to separate occupation and divided old common lands among particular owners, and a standing body of enclosure commissioners was occupied in carrying on the same process. By 1860 some 4000 private-enclosure acts and the activities of the commissioners had within the last century changed 7,000,000 acres from more or less communal to strictly private possession. This had been largely at the expense of the small tenants and farm laborers and had increased the hold of private possessors on the land. Mr. Chamberlain, with some truculence, declared that as a result of having no representation in Parliament the agricultural laborers "have been robbed of their rights in the commons. They have been robbed of their open spaces and are still being robbed. There is no protection against the steady absorption that is continually going on of open spaces which belong to the people, but which are gradually being included in the estates of the landowners." Even as moderate a man as John Stuart Mill declares in this connection, "I confess that I cannot speak of the existing practice of dividing the common land among the landlords by any other name than robbery—robbery of the poor. It will, of course, be said that people cannot be robbed of what is not theirs, and that the commons are not the legal property of the poor. But if the commons are not the property of the poor they are just as little the property of those who take them."

It is true the abolition of the corn laws in 1846 was distasteful to the landowning aristocracy; but it was not an invasion of the rights of private property in land; it was simply the withdrawal of certain subsidies that had previously been given them; it still came under the head of the application of the principles of laissez-faire, in this case to the production of grain and the use of the land.

But with the advance of the century new conditions were coming into existence that brought the question of the control of land to a crisis. Wealth was enclosing more land as deer parks, grouse moors and pleasure grounds. It was making constantly new demands upon previously unused and more or less open ground. The suburbs of the towns were stretching far into the country. At the same time the old wild commons, wolds, moors, forests, and downs, the hunting grounds of kings and the playgrounds of the people from time immemorial, were being closed in by fences. England was fortunate in possessing such tracts, large and small, scattered widely through the island, too sterile to cultivate, covered with rough furze, broom, bracken, and heather, or with a poor growth of hawthorn, oak and other scrub, the resort of wild birds, beasts, and men; the delight of gipsies, loiterers, poets, and writers of romance; of questionable ownership and until recent years in use by every one indiscriminately. Even these were being closed in and put to private use. The open spaces of the country were visibly disappearing.

By 1860, however, the population had risen to 20,000,000. Where should they go for recreation? Except for such small or large spots as each might have claim to, roads, public parks, and the rights of way that were still fortunately guaranteed to the people by the common law, were the only places of refuge from increasing congestion of population. Yet there were those who felt, as was said in Parliament, that consideration must be given to "that which the people of this country want almost as much as food—the air which they breathe and the health which they enjoy." Under these circumstances pressure for the preservation of such open spaces as were left began to appear. Its earliest form was a series of suits in chancery by the community or interested parties to prevent enclosure of open commons, the title to which by the encloser was to say the least tenuous. It was somewhat a matter of surprise that the decisions in these cases so generally upheld the contentions of the commoners against lords of manors who were pushing their rights to enclose. In 1865 the inevitable organization of the advocates of reform took place; the Commons Preservation Society, which still exists, was founded.

During the next decade the influence of this society was helpful in the winning of suit after suit to resist, prevent, or even to reverse the process of enclosure. In the same year as the foundation of this society the House of Commons appointed a committee to investigate the title to all open spaces near London, and in 1872, by the Enclosure of Commons act, the enclosure commissioners were ordered to reverse their former practice of encouragement of enclosures and to disapprove all not to the manifest advantage of the public. The commissioners established park regulations for all open spaces within fifteen miles of London and many other open commons and old forests were transferred to the administration of a public board. Thus Hampstead Heath and Epping Forest and Wimbledon Common and Battersea Park and a series of other open spaces were rescued for the public from private invasion. The jagged edges and little islands of private property that border and lie scattered even yet through these commons testify to the relative suddenness with which the process of their enclosure was stopped. To prohibit the action of a few which leads to the disadvantage of the many is one of the bases of modern reform. Legislation and community action came just in time. It can be seen clearly enough now that less than three-quarters of a century ago the open spaces of England were in grave danger of destruction. Their inestimable value as a possession of the whole English people becomes constantly more clear. The hordes who rush to them for release from the great cities on Sundays and holidays, on railroad trains, busses, and tram cars, testify to this valuation.

There was much to bring the whole question of the land into discussion in this second half of the century. In 1870 the Land Tenure Reform Association was founded by John Stuart Mill and others and began its active campaign. From 1872 to 1874 was the great agricultural laborers' lockout and the formation of the National Union of Agriculture Labourers. In 1874 the report of a government survey which had been made during the last two years at the request of Lord Derby showed that only 2250 persons owned more than half the land of England. In 1879 *Progress and Poverty* was published, and from 1880 to 1882 Henry George was in England, lecturing and disseminating the ideas of that work. In 1882 Alfred Russell Wallace published his *Land Nationalization*; in 1884 the Third Reform bill gave the franchise to the agricultural laborer. There was much emigration abroad and immigration to the city from the country. That the young and vigorous should leave the countryside and only the old, the weak, the unenterprising, and those bound by special circumstances should remain gave a deplorable outlook for the future. How could such depopulation of the countryside be prevented and the people be kept on the land? To many the question took the form; how could more land be brought into the possession of the people? Thus a renewed agitation for either ownership or use of the land by

179

the many began. Jesse Collings, Sir Charles Dilke
and Joseph Chamberlain, all members of Parliament and the last two members of the ministry,
were influential and prominent advocates of land
reform, supporting the efforts of Joseph Arch,
George Edwards, and other representatives of the
laborers or tenants.

As a result of this agitation, in meetings, in
magazines, and in Parliament, a series of acts was
passed along two parallel lines. One was for the
increase of "allotments" to agricultural and other
laborers, the other for the increase of small holdings on which a hard-working farmer might make
a plain living. Allotments were an old institution.
They were pieces of land, usually of less than an
acre, carved out of the arable lands of a neighborhood by parish authorities or landowners, and
rented at the usual rate for agricultural land to
laborers for gardens in which to work after hours
to supplement their wages or to save them from
actual pauperism. They had been advocated and
created at least from the beginning of the century,
had received the distinction of a special essay by
Southey, and the steady though languid support of
the law as a form of poor relief. Now, however,
they were advocated more vigorously, supported
by advanced reformers as a right of the laborers,
as partial recompense for the commons of which
they had been deprived, and in 1882 the Allotments Extension Association was formed. Three
other associations were formed for only slightly

varying objects, the Free Land League, the Leasehold Enfranchisement Association, and the Land Law Reform Association. In 1882 the first Allotments Extension act was passed, largely by the energy of Jesse Collings. Small results followed from a purely permissive act administered by a reluctant class of landowners. In 1887 the reform wing in the new Unionist party, consisting of the same men as had formerly been the advocates of land reform in the old unbroken Liberal party, were able to carry the Labourers' Allotments bill, which gave to the parish authorities the right of compulsory purchase of land for any allotments up to one acre asked for by workingmen, and to acquire by voluntary purchase land for common pasture. In 1890 the act was amended in the direction of greater extension, and in 1894 its administration was handed over to the new democratic parish councils. The number of allotments is a somewhat changing one depending on the demands of laborers and the interest of the authorities. In 1873 there were in existence about 250,000; by 1890 this had risen to 450,000; and it rose to almost 600,000 by 1895. On the outbreak of the Great War in 1914, dread of a food shortage led to their formation in vast numbers, under the pressure of government and public opinion, until there were a million and a half in existence, and whole tracts of England were cut up into checkerboards. After the war their numbers declined and in 1928 there were only 600,000, though there were, at the time of that report, some 14,000 applicants not yet provided for.

Small holdings involved more serious questions, the relative desirability of large and small farms, of ownership and tenancy, the difficulty of obtaining enough land without compelling landowners to sell, and the reluctance of Parliament to authorize compulsion, and all this in a period of serious agricultural depression. English farm tenants and farm laborers show little of that passion for possession of the soil which animates the peasantry of Ireland, France, Russia, and many other countries. Three centuries of landlordism and two of large farming may have habituated them to tenancy and wage labor, or they may by a process of reasoning have decided that the best thing for them is favorable conditions of renting their land. Whatever the cause, the force exerted in favor of recreating a peasant proprietorship or even an extensive system of small tenant farms has come rather from reformers outside of their class than from small farmers themselves. This force has however been steadily and, so far as law is concerned, effectively exerted. The same influential men, organization, and political parties that pressed through the legislation for creating allotments did in the main the same for small farms.

In 1883 an act was passed which gave to the tenant some compensation at the expiry of his lease for improvements he had put upon the land; from 1888 to 1890 a royal commission on Small

Holdings under the presidency of Joseph Chamberlain sat and took evidence, and published its report in 1890. In accordance with the recommendations of this report a law was passed in 1892, providing complete machinery, short of the right of compulsory purchase, for local authorities to create small farms up to fifty acres in size, encourage and help in their purchase, and in default of purchase to rent out farms of ten acres or less to small farmers. These, like allotments, were placed under the parish councils after 1894, and in 1900 a Small Holdings commission was created under the Board of Agriculture by act of Parliament for the further administration of this system.

The success of the creation of a body of small owners or even tenants of agricultural land has been but moderate. Up to 1914 some 12,584 small holders had been established on the land through the intervention, direct or indirect, of Parliament, involving the transfer of about 200,000 acres of land from its former owners. There has been nothing to correspond to the transformation of Ireland from a country of landlords to a country of peasant owners. When in the year 3000 A. D., according to Mr. Shaw in *Back to Methuselah,* an Irish peasant is asked what is meant by a "landlord," he says, "There is a tradition in this part of the country of an animal with a name like that. It used to be hunted and shot in the barbarous ages. It is quite extinct now." In England landlords still exist, if they do not flourish. The breaking up of the large estates as a result of the Great War has proceeded rapidly, but what is to succeed them is not even yet clear.

The great land act of 1928 was intended to codify the land law as it exists, not to introduce any change in it. Nevertheless the land system of England has been completely transformed according to the ideas of reformers and by act of Parliament in the second half of the nineteenth century. The trend toward complete private ownership has been stopped and later reversed. Open spaces have been transferred from semi-private to public ownership and use, much land has been set aside by public authority for the use of workmen after hours, and the legal position of tenants has been much improved, and a class formerly practically excluded from tenancy or ownership of land has now by parliamentary action been admitted to it. Having in view the traditional control of the land by the old aristocracy there is probably no part of the whole domain of public interest where the spirit of reform has shown itself more powerful. Each of the three great political parties has its announced program for the improvement of the condition of the rural classes. They differ in details, rather than in essence, and each party when in power has shown itself slow in carrying the plan out. What the future will show is quite obscure, but whatever it may be, legislation will not be prevented by any great respect for the older "rights of property" or any reluctance to utilize the pow-

184

ers of government in obtaining the desired end.
That contest has already been fought out.

The movement for the better housing of the
working classes in cities and towns passed through
much the same course as legislation for better conditions in the rural districts, and in fact has
reached much the same *impasse.* The population
more than doubled in the first half of the century
and a greatly disproportionate part of this increase
was in cities and towns. As England became more
and more industrial, manufacturing, and commercial, population became more concentrated. Men
must live near their work. Moreover, within the
towns, there was a constant replacement of dwelling sections by manufacturing buildings and offices, railroad stations and yards, and the cutting
through of new streets. It was calculated that between 1860 and 1865, 50,000 people were dis-
placed in this way in London. Workingmen and
their families seldom had the means, the time, or
the enterprise to go far from their accustomed
neighborhood. The result was extreme congestion,
ill housing, and poor sanitation. The conditions
that have been described at the beginning of the
century grew steadily worse. In London and only
to a less extent in the other large cities there were
vast areas of small houses, much subdivided, in
narrow streets and courts, like the parish of St.
Giles in which there were seventy courts, small
streets, and alleyways running into one another,

without access to a single large street. Overcrowding, lack of sunlight, air, and drainage, and high rents forced men down physically, morally, and in economic ability. Even the thrifty and better-paid workmen were often in scarcely better surroundings. The aphorism that "slum people make slums, not slums slum people," if ever true anywhere, was certainly not true in the large English towns of this period. It was rather physical and economic conditions against which the individual was powerless and against which the community had so far taken no action that were responsible.

The laissez-faire attitude, however, gradually passed away. The unsatisfactory living conditions in the towns were manifest to everyone that had eyes to see. It is not a matter of surprise therefore that improved living of the working classes, in the broadened conception of reform, became a familiar object of attention. In fact even before the middle of the century, in 1841, an "Association for Improving the Dwellings of the Industrial Classes" was formed, largely under the kindly influence of Lord Shaftesbury, and it was just after the middle of the century, in 1853, that the first attempt to regulate city building by law was made. This bill, however, was defeated in the House of Lords, and the first serious attempts to meet the difficulty were due to private philanthropy, the Peabody Trust, the Waterlow Company, and the Octavia Hill plan, all of which were inaugurated between 1860 and 1865. Their object was rather the provision of better dwellings for workingmen than a direct attack on congestion. Even the first legislation, the Artisans' and Labourers' Dwellings act, the so-called "Torrens act," of 1868, only empowered city authorities by voluntary agreement with the owner to pull down unfit houses and replace them by new.

It was obvious that these means, however beneficial to those who profited by them, were quite ineffective as a solution of the general problem, for up to 1875 but 30,000 persons had been provided with satisfactory dwellings in London, whereas the increase of population in that city was 40,000 a year, an appreciable proportion of whom were slum dwellers. The pressure for doing something was however very strong, the report of Shuttleworth to the Charity Organization Society in 1873 being particularly outspoken in its demands for government action. In 1875 therefore under Mr. Disraeli's government the Housing of the Artisan and Working Classes act made it incumbent upon city authorities to condemn dwelling sections, where existing conditions were especially unsatisfactory, take them over by compulsory purchase, and erect new houses. Other acts followed upon this, and in 1890 a general codifying act was passed. There has been no lack of attempts at reform in this field; it is a typical instance of acceptance by all of the need and propriety of social reform directed by government. If not much has been accomplished, if the problem has not been yet solved, it is because of its extreme difficulty or because it cannot be solved except after a still fuller acceptance of social control.

The culmination of constructive social reform during this period is to be found in the group of laws placed upon the statute book in the years from 1906 to the outbreak of the Great War by the combination of efforts of the Liberal, Labour, and Irish Nationalist parties. During these eight years a greater body of reform legislation was passed than in any earlier similar stretch of time. Neither the years from 1832 to 1836, the period of the first parliamentary reform bill and its resultant legislation, nor the years from 1868 to 1874, Mr. Gladstone's "great administration," can compare with its achievements in far-reaching reforming legislation. The old familiar power of the House of Lords, used to block advanced social legislation, was taken away from them, and at the same time a notable step toward democracy was taken by the payment of salaries to the members of the House of Commons, who might now more readily be workingmen. New principles of taxation, asserting the right of the state to look into the sources as well as to estimate the amount of the taxpayers' income, and to use taxation as a means of redressing some of the inequalities of the competitive system, were introduced into the annual budget. Trade unions were finally legalized and protected against economic as well as against criminal prosecution, and their powers extended. Workmen's compensation, housing and town plan-

ning and development obtained the full acceptance and extension already described. A series of
"Children's acts" did much to make the mass of
school children veritable wards of the state.

Four great reforms met or attempted to meet,
one after another, as many of the fundamental
needs of the lower ranges of society, support in
old age, relief in sickness, regular occupation, a
living wage. For these ends old age pensions were
provided, labor exchanges for securing employment were established, trade boards were appointed
for setting authoritative rates of wages in poorly
paid industries, and national insurance in sickness
and time of unemployment was introduced. The
objects of these acts are sufficiently clear. The main
questions, so far as this work is concerned, are
how such far-reaching and fundamental laws
came to be adopted, and what light their adoption
throws on the general trend of reform. It may be
observed that most of these projects had long
been ripe for action; the driving force to carry
them through alone was lacking. For instance, all
parties had accepted the necessity for some support of the aged other than private philanthropy
or the poor law afforded. The Old Age Pension act
of 1908, only gave special shape to a plan already
more than half approved, and the million old men
and women who were drawing pensions under it
by the year of the outbreak of the war would probably have received them from any party which
happened to be in power. When an old woman of

sixty-four now remarks, "I'll get my Lloyd George next year," she is paying tribute to the chancellor of the exchequer who but chanced at that time to be the champion of aged indigence.

The inclusion of seamen, domestic servants, and government employes in the system of compulsory compensation for accident and industrial disease in 1906 was an extension of the Workmen's Compensation act of 1898; the passage of such an act had already been attempted by the Conservatives in 1905. The threat to the funds of the trade unions involved in the Taff Vale decision alarmed Conservatives and Liberals, as well as rousing the apprehension of the Labour party. The Conservative party itself introduced, though it was not successful in carrying, a bill to protect trade-union funds from suits. It was an extension of the principle of this bill which was embodied in the Trade Disputes act of 1906 and the Trade Union act of 1913. A long series of parliamentary investigations of wages, from 1892 forward, the activities of the Anti-sweating League and successive bills concerning wages introduced into Parliament from 1895 to 1905 found their completion, not their initiation, in the Trade Boards act of 1909. The early example of Germany and somewhat later of other continental countries had long suggested the compulsory sickness and unemployment insurance plans introduced by the act of 1911.

The debates were rather on the details than on the principles of these measures. Nevertheless, although the greater part of this reforming legislation of 1906–1914 had been proposed and even prepared for before, it was the peculiar combination of progressive elements in the grouping of parties in that period and their domination by a few bold reforming spirits that brought that body of legislation actually to the birth. A ministry which could count for progressive legislation on 378 Liberals, 83 Irish Nationalists and 53 Labour members, altogether 514 votes, against an opposition of only 156 was all-powerful and needed only leadership to carry reform far forward. If any Parliament ever had a mandate to experiment in social progress and the power to carry it out, it was the Parliament that met in 1906. The principal ministers were deeply pledged to reform. Mr. Asquith, chancellor of the exchequer, declared in Parliament in 1907, "Beyond there lies the whole still unconquered territory of social reform. . . . This is a House of Commons which was elected more clearly and definitely than any other House in our history in the hope and belief on the part of the electors that it would find the road and provide the means for social reform . . . there is nothing that calls so loudly or so imperiously as the possibilities of social reform."

Lloyd George when in a similar position in 1909, introducing his budget demanding large appropriations for old age pensions, insurance, and administrative expenses, in addition to military and naval requirements, declared: "There are hundreds of thousands of men, women and children in this country, now enduring hardships for which the sternest judge would not hold them responsible; hardships entirely due to circumstances over which they have not the slightest control. . . . Is it fair, is it just, is it humane, is it honorable, is it safe to subject such a multitude of our poor fellow-countrymen and countrywomen to continued endurance of these miseries until nations have learned enough wisdom not to squander their resources on these huge machines for the destruction of life? This is a war budget. It is for raising money to wage implacable warfare against poverty or squalidness. I cannot help hoping and believing that before this generation has passed away we shall have advanced a great step towards that good time when poverty and wretchedness and human degradation which always follow in its camp will be as remote to the people of this country as the wolves which once infested its forests." When such views were held by the leading ministers it is no wonder that these measures were pushed at last to completion. If there was any flagging on the part of the Liberals, they were urged to their task by the Labour members, whose support was so important to the ministry, and by the Nationalists who were not only well inclined to reform but were anxious to bring these projects to completion so that attention might be given to their own more special desires. The dark shadow of the war had not yet settled down on the country, England as a whole was rich and prosperous, however dire the need for a better distribution of its prosperity, and men generally believed with Lloyd George that poverty could be exorcised by appropriate reform measures. So as the principal work of the eight years a good baker's dozen of new laws were passed, each carrying some old and hopeful line of reform a long step forward or initiating a new and still more hopeful effort to bring about social welfare. The work was only brought to a close by the catastrophe of war.

The trend of reforming legislation from the beginning of the last century to the Great War is by this time sufficiently clear. Its progress has been from the meager gifts of a kindly if somewhat frigid justice, wrested by upper-class reformers from a stolid Parliament and bestowed upon a few victims of servitude, misfortune, crime, or poverty, to constructive laws given openhandedly by a democratic Parliament to the whole or a great part of the population. Reform has passed from the slight and grudging deviation from the principle of laissez faire of a hesitant Parliament to the aphorism of a recent prime minister that "political machinery is only valuable and is only worth having as it is adapted to and used for worthy social ends." It has shifted from the few to the many, from negative to positive, from abolition of old abuses to creation of new institutions, from things done by some for others to things done for all by all.

This development has followed, as indicated at

the beginning of this book, an inner law of its own. It has been largely independent of political parties. Although Whigs and Liberals have been on the whole rather more willing to pass reform measures than Tories and their successors, Conservatives and Unionists, yet these measures have been pretty equally attributable to both parties. The first law legalizing trade unions, that of 1824–25, was passed by the Conservatives, the law of 1871 by the Liberals, that of 1875 by the Conservatives, that of 1906 again by the Liberals. The Employers' Liability act of 1880 was adopted by a Liberal, the Workmen's Compensation act of 1897 by a Conservative Parliament. The fountainhead of factory legislation is to be found in a strictly Tory Parliament, in 1802, its main principles were accepted under Conservative ministers in the forties and the Factory and Workshop Consolidation act of 1878 was also the work of a Conservative administration. On the other hand later developments in that field have been under Liberal auspices. Land reform has been on the whole the work of Liberal majorities, but some of the most important acts were passed by Unionists and Conservatives between 1880 and 1890.

Some of the reasons for this development irrespective of parties are obvious. Propagandist bodies have been usually non-partisan and their work of conversion has been done in both parties alike. The royal and even the parliamentary commissions of investigation whose reports have been so influential in producing legislation have included men

from all parties and men without known party af-
filiation, and they have often reported, moreover, in
the frequent changes of English politics, to a Parliament with a different majority from that under
which they were appointed. There have been natural
reformers in high position, Peel, Gladstone, Disraeli, Chamberlain, Lloyd George, in all parties.
Social legislation has been largely a response to
pressure from outside of Parliament and party organizations, and whatever party was in power when
this pressure became sufficiently strong has performed the work of placing it upon the statute book.
For the ultimate and efficient causes of reform,
search must be made much deeper in society than the
ups and downs in the strife of political parties.

All of the reforms so far described, both those
that came early and those that came late, have been
detached reforms, each directed toward the removal of some special abuse, the alleviation of some
particular form of suffering, or the establishment of
some distinctive beneficial practice. The activity of
reformers, so far as we have traced it, has consisted
in taking up one object of social reform after another and securing legislation upon it, partially
and tentatively or boldly and constructively, yet in
neither case with any general plan including all
needed or desirable reforms. Running like a slender
stream parallel to the main river of reform through
the whole century has been a quite different ideal.
This has been the advocacy of some fundamental
change in social organization that would produce the

same results and many more by a single transforming process. Such a change would preclude the
necessity for separate reforms by introducing one
general all-inclusive reform. Such a proposed deliberate remodelling of society is, of course, socialism, which has been urged in one form or another
continuously through the nineteenth century, and
has already put a perceptible impress upon legislation. This proposal and its relation to the general
course of reform will be the subject of the next
and concluding chapter.

# VI

## BRITISH SOCIALISM, 1817–1930

WHEN in July 1817 Robert Owen laid before
a committee of the House of Commons on
the Poor Laws his plan for setting people to work
in groups to fulfil one another's needs instead of
either being supported in idleness or working for
wages to produce goods to be sold in the open market,
he started British socialism on its career as a
practical plan for the general reform of society. He
proposed that either the government or interested
committees or persons should buy or rent tracts
of land, each of sufficient extent to produce food
for a thousand or fifteen hundred or more persons;
that on such a tract should be erected dwellings,
farm and factory buildings, a school and amusement hall, and all the other needs for the life of a
group of people who should live to a great extent
coöperatively, supplying their joint needs and producing enough surplus for some trading and for the
ultimate repayment of the costs of establishing the
community. In this way those now unemployed
would find occupation and sustenance, and the cost
and demoralizing effect of their support by taxes
or charity be avoided. In their concrete form, such

"villages of coöperation," as he called them, of which he made drawings and later plaster models, with calculations of exact numbers of inhabitants, cost and productions, seem fantastic enough. But the plan was drawn up, in the first place, as a device for solving the pressing problem of unemployment and poverty, and it was only later that he conceived of it as furnishing a model for a general transformation of society. Owen himself was a practical man, experienced, traveled, with a wide and varied circle of acquaintances, wealthy and of illimitable energy. An early nineteenth century Henry Ford, he had the peculiar combination of business acumen with imagination not unusual in the higher type both of business men and idealists. The parliamentary committee, dominated by the prevailing laissez-faire and dissuaded from any interference with competitive business by the influential rising manufacturers, would not even listen to Owen's plans, and although he appealed to the public through the newspapers and successive pamphlets, of which he circulated forty thousand free copies, spending £4000 in two months, his stereotyped village community received more ridicule than acceptance.

The real significance of his proposal was in the principles upon which it was based. This and later schemes with which Owen was connected in his long lifetime of business organization, public agitation, writing, and speaking, arose from two fundamental conceptions, one economic, the other psy-

chological. Although himself a participant in and
beneficiary of the Industrial Revolution, he was
doubtful of its benefits. He was a successful mill-
owner, one of the group of men of enterprise who
seized the opportunity offered by the new inventions, the pressing demands of the market, the
abundance of available capital, and the ample labor
supply to build up for themselves, for their part-
ners, and for England great industrial establishments and great wealth. He differed, however, from
most of the "cotton lords" in being a man of ideas
beyond those required for successful business. He
was early alarmed at the possibility, indeed before
many years impressed with the realization of men
being thrown out of work by the new inventions in
spinning and other industries—"technological unemployment" as it is called in modern discussions.
In this he found the cause of the widespread misery
after 1815 that led to his first socialistic proposal,
"a scientific arrangement of the people united in
properly constructed villages of unity and co-
operation."

He calculated that the productive power of Great
Britain in 1817, with its 17,000,000 inhabitants,
having now the use of machinery and other improvements in production, was as great as it would be if
it had a population of 200,000,000 using manual
labor alone. The productive powers had increased
tenfold. Since men are more expensive than machines, unless there is some regulation what is to
save them, in the exigencies of competition, from

being constantly superseded by machines? "Increase of mechanical power is constantly diminishing the demand for and value of manual labor." If capitalists endowed with the new mechanical powers are to be allowed to produce without any limitation except their own individual profit, the new machinery, capital, and enterprise will be a curse to the bulk of mankind, the source of demoralization, misery, and conflict. This condition, because it has been created by man's inventions, is an artificial condition. "This new and artificial state of society, . . . our most irrational system of creating wealth," cannot safely be let alone. "The artificial law of supply and demand, arising from the principle of individual gain," is, under the new circumstances, "in opposition to the well being of society." It brings with it, when unregulated, various evils—unemployment, "the deteriorating condition of the young children and others who have been made the slaves of these new mechanical powers." Uncontrolled mechanical production is an artificial evil, to be met, like all artificial ills by remedies. The remedy for some of its evils is to be found in a factory law, like the one he initiated in 1815 which resulted in the emasculated statute of 1819; or it may require an "arrangement formed by society purposely devised to give employment to all who are competent and willing to labor." It is the belief that industrialism is in itself fraught with evils; that it must, for the good of society, be subjected to control, that primarily makes Owen a socialist.

This readiness to accept control arose however from Owen's other and still more fundamental ruling conception. He had formulated to himself, "discovered," he called it, what he considered a great truth, that people are what they have been made by the circumstances that have surrounded them. "Men's characters are made for them not by them," according to his thousand-times-reiterated formula. Men and society are therefore plastic and can be given whatever shape their leaders, teachers, and rulers desire. Regulation and regimentation are easy and will be effective. He claims to have proved this by his experience in creating his model factory village, New Lanark. Over and over again, from every point of view, he states and restates his belief that men are absolutely and entirely the product of their environment. Philosophers and theologians and statesmen are and always have been on a false track in holding men responsible for what they do and what they are; we should turn our energies to educating men and surrounding them with good influences, so that they will do what they ought to do. "Human nature is radically good, and is capable of being trained, educated and placed from birth in such manner that all ultimately must become united, good, wise, wealthy and happy."

It was however neither the specific plans that Owen advocated, several of which were tried with but ill success, nor his belief that one generation can carve the next into any shape it desires, which convinced but few, nor even his wealth and devotion, which were used unsparingly in his causes, that made "Owenism" a widely acting force in England in his time and a force in all modern socialism. It was rather his conviction that what there was dangerous in modern industrialism could be guarded against by deliberate regulation and, this having been done, all mankind might by their own efforts become comfortable, kindly and happy. Socialism, as he taught it, was a gospel of hope for all. Individualism was false doctrine; competition was bound to bring misery to many; coöperation was founded in human nature and if once applied would bring prosperity to all.

Between 1815 and 1845 such ideas, though but a small barrier to the overwhelming acceptance and advance of competitive industry and sentiment, spread through the community, appealed to many minds, and induced some to enter upon practical projects; among them the Rochdale Pioneers, the creators of the modern consumers' coöperative movement. During this period the word "socialism" came into common use as descriptive of opposition to competition as a rule of economic action and legislation, the first use of the term, so far as observed, having been a rather casual one, in the Coöperative Magazine in 1827. There was a certain socialistic or coöperative element in Chartism, although its economic and social objects were necessarily subordinated to its struggle for political ends. A declaration made in 1843 that "Socialism and Chartism pursue the same aims, they only differ in their methods," is essentially true, though the pursuit of socialist aims at that time was certainly languid, while the Chartists were hot in pursuit of universal suffrage and the other political points of the Charter.

After about 1845 interest in socialism as a general proposal for the reorganization of society goes under a cloud, from which it scarcely emerges for forty years. It is true that Maurice, Kingsley, and their friends, in advocating coöperation in 1848 were called and called themselves "Christian Socialists," criticized the employing manufacturers, and taught that "human society is a body consisting of many members, not a collection of warring atoms. A principle of justice, not of selfishness, must govern exchanges," all of which is good socialist doctrine. The Christian Socialists however were, as has been said of them, "leaders and officers but without any army behind them," and the cult gradually died out. It is also true that the "Communist Manifesto," the first formulation in popular language of Marxian socialism, and the storehouse of a new vocabulary and a new group of conceptions, "exploitation," "class struggle," "bourgeoisie," "proletariat," "revolution," and internationalism, was written and published in England, in German, in February 1848. But it was not put into English until 1851, it was the product of foreigners living in England rather than of Englishmen, and its echoes for a long time were on the Continent, not in England.

Socialism came to be looked upon, notwithstanding its purely English origin and the early prevalence of socialist ideals in England, as an exotic on English soil. Carlisle might declare that "Laissez-faire, laissez-passer, as a principle, is false, heretical and damnable, if ever aught was." Southey might look forward to the abolition of poverty as a great reform, just as men had abolished slavery, and to community of land taking the place of its aggregation in the hands of a few great landowners. Dr. Arnold protested against the maxim that "civil society ought to leave its members alone each to look after their several interests." Ruskin and Dickens are scarcely ever weary of pointing out that society on a purely competitive basis is ill-founded, unjust, and destructive to happiness. Even John Stuart Mill says, in his *Autobiography*, "I look forward to a time when . . . the division of the produce of labor . . . will be made by concert on an acknowledged principle of justice."

But these criticisms of existing conditions were negative, not positive; socialism contemplates a new organization of society, not merely a dissatisfied attitude toward present society. As a matter of fact, in the middle decades of the nineteenth century, intellectual, well-to-do, and advanced reformers were satisfied with the ideals of liberalism; the workingmen's leaders, occupied with the building up of their trade unions, the securing of the ballot, coöperation, and recurring temperance crusades and religious revivals, had little in-

terest left for any such general reform as socialism. It may be that the English type of mind was
unresponsive to general ideas and found little appeal in proposals for a complete transformation of
society. Whatever may have been the cause, socialism remained but a slender thread in the skein of
English thought and discussion, and, while strong
socialist political parties were growing up on the
continent and international socialism was taking
shape, socialism awakened in England, between
1850 and 1880, none of that robust interest so widely
shown in individual reforms.

After 1880 it was different. The great current of
continental socialism set, partially at least, into
England; Liberal and Conservative reforming tendencies, except when whipped up from the outside,
had about run their course, Times were hard;
foreign competition pressed on English industrial
predominance and there was much unemployment.
Workingmen were forced to think about or at least
to listen to proposals for more far-reaching changes
than those that have made up the principal subject
of the preceding chapters of this book. Socialism,
whether by its own name or in essence, now becomes
a great underlying influence upon the progress of
reform.

It may be conducive to clearness to conceive of
socialism as attacking the citadel of purely competitive society during this period by a threefold
advance. The earliest approach was the entrance of
government upon the field of industry. Of course,

government had carried on the post office from time immemorial and had engaged in certain industries due to its military, naval, and financial requirements. In 1861 Mr. Gladstone, when President of the Board of Trade established the Post Office Savings Bank, and in 1864 encouraged the trade unions to deposit their funds in it. He had certainly no realization that he was involving the government in a new policy; government was nevertheless embarking upon the banking business. In 1880 the sale of annuities through the post office was begun, thus entering upon that insurance business which has since been carried so far, in the form of sickness and unemployment insurance. In 1883 the Parcel Post was instituted, the first step toward a government monopoly of the express business. In the seventies and eighties government took over the telegraph and telephone lines. In 1890 it began the acquisition by compulsory purchase of insanitary dwellings to be demolished and replaced by better workingmen's houses, thus entering upon the field of real estate development. Just before the war the Road and Development Committee was created by act of Parliament for the purpose of carrying out drainage and afforesting schemes, harbor improvements, the building of inter-municipal railways, the encouragement of fisheries, and the establishment of certain minor industries. Parallel with these early and mostly unconscious intrusions of the national government into the fields of transportation, insurance, building, and general indus-

trial development there was a corresponding establishment by municipalities and county governments
of tramways and ferries, gas and water works, laun-
dries, restaurants and slaughter houses. These were
none the less government-owned because the government was local, not national. As these early
steps of government and municipal ownership are
now looked back upon they are easily perceived
to have been, however they looked to those then
advocating them, all in the direction of the limitation of the field of competitive business, the socialization of certain activities previously left to private
competitors.

During the war government ownership made
enormous strides. The day after the declaration of
war the twenty-nine railroads of the country were
taken over and during the war administered by a
government official. Factories suitable for the manu-
facture of munitions and army and navy supplies
became government establishments. Wool, hides, and
leather were taken by compulsory purchase, mines
were subjected to government control and all shipping made subservient to the immediate needs of
government.

It is true that most of these industries and
processes of distribution were seized for war purposes, an old function of government, and that they
were returned to their former owners when the
war was over. But socialists and some others protested against the return, and it gave occasion to
everyone to realize how many are the links between

government and business, and how easy would be the transition from private to government control. Men might readily reason in future that what was good in time of war might be good in time of peace, and that any superiority of private over government ownership was merely a problem of administration, not a question of principle. For most of the period since the war conditions have not been favorable to the enlargement of the sphere of government owner-ship. There has been however a steady increase in its bulk, and under the stimulus of unemployment the old process of extension into new fields has already begun. Something over a million men and women, almost one-tenth of all persons receiving wages in England, are in the employ of government. It has been recently calculated that one-tenth of all the business of the country is in the hands of govern-ment, and that if this were capitalized, the amount would be about $12,500,000,000. So far has in-dustry carried on by government superseded indus-try carried on by private parties. This alteration from private to public industry is obviously social-istic. So far as it has extended, rent, profits, and in-terest have disappeared. Government employees are not seeking profit for themselves or the government, they are working for a salary paid by the commu-nity for service to the community. Government ownership, whether national or local, is commu-nity ownership, and if it should be carried to its full extent, would bring in the socialist state. All men would be serving the people through the government, as are postmen and other civil servants and soldiers now, and all would be drawing their support from the community. The growth of government ownership is the most spontaneous form in which the modern trend toward socialism has shown itself.

A second form of approach is to be found in the socialistic element in recent humanitarian legislation. Such legislation has been increasingly based on the recognition that the competitive form of society is ineffective for general prosperity and social justice. The alleviation of various ills provided in this legislation is at the expense not only of the national treasury but of the theory of individualism. This is especially true of the social reforms already alluded to, adopted in the decade just before the war, when the Liberal, Labour and Nationalist parties combined to introduce by parliamentary action old age pensions, labor exchanges, trade boards, and national insurance. When government took over the support of all aged workingmen and workingwomen, it was on the assumption that under a competitive system wages are not ordinarily sufficient to provide savings for old age or for the support of their aged parents by young working people. Something is being returned to old people which they probably earned by their earlier labor but had not been paid. They are, as a matter of fact, what they were called in debate, "veterans of industry." They have the same claim to support by the community as other incapacitated veterans who have

209

helped to create or maintain the present condition of affairs political or economic.

Government labor exchanges have been established because labor is not sufficiently fluid to permit of employers and employees finding one another without the intervention of the state. The deficiencies of private business in this respect are therefore made good by the action of the government. The legally enforceable wages that are now insured to about a million workers by the Trade Boards act are an acknowledgment that a living wage would not be paid in these industries if left to competition alone; in these industries therefore regulation of wages through legislation has superseded competition. Compulsory unemployment insurance is based on the well-known experience that employers are not able to provide unbroken employment. A case might be made out for the same responsibility of the employers to pay wages to their regular employees as they have to pay interest on their loans or dividends on their capital. This is impossible under purely competitive conditions, and the community has therefore offered its help in providing for this one of the ordinary exigencies of industrial life, by making out-of-work insurance compulsory and by assisting in paying its expenses.

These reforms have a twofold interest; they not only alleviate present distress but they appear to be first steps in the direction of a much greater change. They imply that the causes of distress are fundamental in our present industrial system, and suggest some degree of transformation. It is not a matter of wonder therefore that their socialistic implications have been recognized both by sympathizers and opponents. "Tentative, doctrineless socialism," they are called by one of the former. One of the latter, Lord Derby, speaking in opposition to the Old Age Pension act, remarks "I think my friends are moving in the path that leads toward socialism." They are both right. Laws implying the infeasibility of attaining general prosperity under a competitive system and establishing regulation by government in its stead could be carried to any length without further change of principle. Thus the second approach to socialism is to be found in the far-reaching social legislation of recent times.

So we come to the third of the converging lines of socialistic influence on the reform movement. This is socialism known as such, teaching its doctrines, claiming support and urging action under it own name or some recognized equivalent of that name. It was in the troubled decade between 1880 and 1890 that the first two active and lasting modern socialist bodies, the Social Democratic Federation and the Fabian Society were established. Their members were for the most part literary men, like Shaw, Wells, and Hyndman, or artists, like Morris and Crane, or teachers, such as Webb and Wallas. Both continued to be in the main composed of "intellectuals," strong in education, abilities, and position, weak in numbers. They were as dissatisfied with existing conditions as were, or had been, Carlyle, Ruskin and many other early critics of society, but they differed from them in having a definite plan for improving it, and to this plan they set about converting England. Those who sought immediate results and were willing to take forcible measures, if necessary and practicable,—genuine "Marxists,"—formed the Social Democratic Federation, which after successive changes of name is now the British Socialist party. Others,—"revisionists,"—believing in the necessity for persuasion and for gradual, even if ultimately complete change, formed the Fabian Society.

The leading ideas of socialism, through their efforts and other means, percolated downward and spread widely. The first popular response to this influence was the formation in 1892 of the Independent Labour Party. This was a group of workingmen leaders who had tried unsuccessfully to induce the annual Trade Union Congress to enter as a party into politics and to declare for a socialistic platform. The Independent Labour Party may be defined as a socialist group of workingmen, striving to gain their ends by political action. It was in a certain sense a revival of the Chartism of three-quarters of a century before, though the old political ends having now been mostly reached, their objects extended further into the field of actual change. They were from the beginning satisfied with a "revisionist" attitude, their leaders having little to say about "the class war," "the revolution," or the "dictatorship of the proletariat." On the other hand they were impatient for some immediate action and it was this group that were responsible somewhat later for the cry "socialism in our time." Their success in parliamentary elections was slight, indeed they were not able for some time to win any seats, as a party, though some of the workingmen members of Parliament were socialists by conviction. On the other hand their principal leaders, Keir Hardie, James Ramsay MacDonald, Tom Mann, Philip Snowden, J. R. Clynes, Robert Smillie and others were popular and influential speakers and in some cases writers, and the new party elected many members of town and county councils.

In 1899 the basis was at last laid for a party that should be at once numerous and socialist. This was the adoption by a small majority by the Trade Union Congress of that year of a resolution instructing its executive committee to invite all coöperative and socialist societies, trade unions and other working-class bodies to unite in an organization for the purpose of increasing the number of workingmen's representatives in Parliament. Early in the next year this conference was held. The party was there formed which soon adopted the name of the Labour party. The new party was not at first a socialist party, as many, perhaps a majority, of its trade-union members were not yet socialists. On the other hand its most vigorous leaders were socialists, the socialist weekly newspapers were widely read by its members, and in its discussions socialism was proclaimed by the speakers as its ultimate goal. "We socialists think," "it is the aim of all of us who are socialists," and similar expressions were familiar in the discussions of the party from the beginning. The Labour party might be considered as practically a socialist party after the annual conference of 1908, when a resolution was adopted "that in the opinion of this Conference the time has arrived when the Labour party should have as a definite object the socialization of the means of production, distribution and exchange, to be controlled by a democratic state in the interest of the entire community."

Even before the war, then, socialism had become a large factor in thought, legislation, and discussion on reform. It was unacknowledged, but none the less existent, in the gradual extension of government ownership in the field of industry; involved in laws looked upon primarily as lenitives, but essentially subversive of individualism; widely accepted as a creed and embodied in at least one political party of rapidly growing numbers.

Then came the war, with its intensification of all emotions, its embitterment of social conflicts, its questioning of interests and objects; the extensive, if temporary, adoption of state socialism already described; government control over food supply, prices, wages, and profits; the adulation of the working classes as those who alone could carry the country through the crisis, and consequent promises much easier to make than to fulfil. And close upon the war came the Communist revolution in Russia. The repercussion of the Russian revolution

in England was threefold. It drove many into reactionary fear of sudden social change or even the
overthrow of established institutions, strengthened
conservatism and, like the French revolution more
than a century before, hardened opposition to any
extended reforms or any coöperation with continental radicalism. On the other hand, it filled some
men with enthusiasm. They saw socialism now a
reality, not merely a dream; an actually existing
form of government, putting the proposals of Marx
into force, so far as possible in the conditions of the
time in Russia and as an immediate policy. So the
small British Communist party was born and has
continued, though with few adherents since.

But the most distinctive influence of the war and
of Bolshevism was to force socialists, and specifically the Labour party, to clarify their principles
and aims. They needed to distinguish their position
from that of the Communists on the one hand and
the Conservatives and Liberals on the other. So a
special conference of the Labour party, meeting in
January 1918, adopted the statement of principles
known as "Labour and the New Social Order." The
twenty-point program on which the campaign of
the Labour party was fought in 1918; "Labour
and the Nation," the platform of the party in 1928,
"The Constitution of a Socialist State," the answer
of Sidney and Beatrice Webb to the challenge that
socialists should describe more clearly what they
proposed to substitute for the present system, differed from the pronouncement of 1918 only in be-

ing more concrete in their proposals. It is from these documents that can be derived the predominating characteristics of modern British socialism so far as that is embodied in the Labour party.

It is gradual, not revolutionary. According to the platform of 1928 "these tasks, one after another, the more pressing and important being dealt with first of all, must be undertaken by a Labour party in power, and every parliamentary opportunity used to settle them." That is to say the reorganization of society they propose is to come step by step; the transition is to be "without disorder or confusion, with the consent of the majority of the electors and by the use of the ordinary machinery of democratic government." Parliament as it stands is good enough for their purposes, though they would probably introduce proportional representation on an industrial basis, and would certainly abolish the House of Lords; the monarchy is apparently not especially distasteful to the majority of English socialists, though an appreciable number would prefer a republic. However gradually the party should carry out its ideals it is uncompromisingly socialist. "The Labour party is a socialist party." "The Labour party is concerned with transforming capitalism into socialism." It judges the present capitalist system harshly; speaks of its "reckless profiteering and wage slavery," of "the monstrous inequality of circumstances that it produces," the "degradation and brutalization, both moral and spiritual resulting therefrom." It declares that we have al-

lowed the riches of our mines, the rental value of
unusually productive lands, the extra profits of
especially fortunate capitalists and the material outcome of scientific discoveries to be absorbed by individual proprietors and "devoted very largely to
the senseless luxury of an idle rich class." It describes present industry as "a jostling crowd of
separate private employers, with their minds bent,
not on the service of the community, but, by the
very law of their being, only on the utmost possible
profiteering."

For this condition of almost unregulated competition among private or joint-stock capitalists they
would substitute "a genuinely scientific reorganization of the nation's industry, no longer deflected by
individual profiteering, on the basis of the common ownership of the means of production and the
equitable sharing of the proceeds among all who
participate in any capacity, and only among these."
It is not, according to their claim, a class scheme.
"All workers by hand or brain" are admitted to all
the advantages and powers of society as it is to
be ultimately reconstructed, and liberal provision
will be made for the unfortunate and the aged; for
hospitals, education, parks, galleries, libraries,
music, and scientific research. Nor is the socialistic
Labour party predatory; property taken over will
be with compensation to present owners. But ultimately there will be no opportunity to live on
rent, interest, or profits; they will all have disappeared, all income except for dependents will be

in the form of salaries for service. The national or municipal government will be the sole employer; mines, railroads, power, insurance, banks, and all other fundamental and eventually all industries will be administered, each according to its peculiar requirements, in the interest of the whole community, without private capital or profits. The ultimate objects of this socialist party of the twentieth century are not very different from the hopeful visions of the Utopian socialists of the early nineteenth, or the bitter creed of the Marxian socialists of the middle of that century. It is its gradual methods, its realism, and what appears to be its favorable opportunity that are different. For each recent parliamentary election has seen an increase in its numbers. In 1918 it had two and a quarter million votes, in 1922 and 1923 it had some four and a quarter, in 1924 it had five and a half and in 1929 it had something over eight million votes.

Its leaders have been twice in office though not with a parliamentary majority. The party is not all socialist, but its leaders are so almost without exception, and doubtless the great majority of its voters. Small impress of formal socialism has so far been placed upon legislation; whether because of the absence of a clear majority in Parliament, or because of the unfavorable circumstances of the time, or because of its fundamental difficulty, or because of the half-heartedness of the ministers or from some other cause. But the announced and intended projects of the party are clear and unquestionable.

218

It is socialism about to enter upon its inheritance, even if that inheritance is somewhat postponed.

In the meantime some other forms of socialism have asserted themselves, the most pervasive of which is probably what is known as "gild socialism." With the conviction that a man's labor is or should be inseparable from his personality, and not therefore a commodity, such as capital or land or raw materials, it was reasoned that the use made of a man's labor should be controlled by himself, not by an employer. The gild socialists declare that the wage system is fundamentally a wrong system, and that the failure of specific reforms and of other types of socialism to make the mass of men more prosperous is due to a failure to recognize this and to act accordingly. During the years just before the war and during the war, when such numerous social reforms were being carried through Parliament, and when the Labour party was developing its principles of state socialism, a number of men of intellectual interests were pouring out a flood of books advocating the abolition of the wage system, the establishment of self-government in industry by the workers themselves, and the foundation of a number of "national gilds" to take over and administer the various industries. In 1915 was founded on these lines the "National Gilds League." They have never drawn to themselves any great numbers, but their ideas have spread widely in trade unions, in other socialist bodies, and among the professional and leisured classes.

However unfavorable to socialistic experimentation have been economic conditions since the war, they have not been adverse to socialistic thinking. The "Liberal Inquiry into England's Industrial Future" drawn up by a number of prominent industrial leaders and others influential in the Liberal party, declares that "The distinction between Individualism and Socialism is obsolete." Although this is an exaggerated statement, the conditions the "Inquiry" describes are certainly little to the credit of competitive society. "No impartial man would contend that our industrial system has yet attained an adequate standard either of justice or of efficiency . . . it still allows a mass of great poverty at the one end, at the other an ostentatious luxury which is bitterly and rightly resented. For several years a million of our working people have been unemployed; a large additional number have been living as best they could on the low earnings of short time and intermittent work. In spite of the building of numbers of new houses, the slums of the great cities remain almost as they were; from overcrowding and the ill health and degradation that come from it, millions of the people are still powerless to escape. Yet all the time individuals accumulate or inherit great fortunes, and it is clear in all men's sight that, more often than not, the prizes are awarded capriciously, with little regard either to economic service or to personal desert."

If these views may be attributed to leaders of the Liberals, who are mostly of the employing class, it is not a matter of surprise that the corresponding views of workingmen, gathered from their declaration at the Joint Industrial Conference called by the government in 1919, should be still more critical of present conditions. "The fundamental cause of labor unrest lies not so much in any detailed grievances as in the growing opposition of labor to the whole existing structure of capitalist industry; the belief of the working class that production for profit is a bad basis for society. . . . Labor has grown too strong to remain within the bounds of the old industrial system. . . . It is not enough merely to tinker with particular grievances or to endeavor to reconstruct the old system by slight adjustments. . . . It is essential to question the whole basis on which our industry has been conducted in the past, to substitute for the motive of private gain the motive of public service." These are, however carefully the term may be avoided, the ideals of socialism.

It would seem therefore that there is in many men's minds a new and more thorough-going conception of reform. It contemplates not separate improvements, but a complete, even though a gradual reorganization of society. The same reforms, or extensions of them, might, under this ideal, be advocated as have been urged in the past, but they would be thought of as part of a general plan. Some changes might be recommended which would do little to remove any special evil, but which would help bring into existence a condition of affairs in which that and other evils would disappear. Never again perhaps will a measure of reform be introduced into Parliament without considering whether it is a logical part of a general system of reform. If the reforms of the early nineteenth century were mere removal of conspicuous abuses, if those of the latter half of the century were detached steps toward social justice, those of the twentieth century bid fair to be influenced deeply by the notion of a deliberate transformation.

We are thus brought in our narrative to the very threshold of the present. We are not called on to prophesy, but we may stand at this point of vantage and, as we have traced the trend of social reform in the past, we may peer a little way into the future and see its probable nature and direction. There is every reason to believe that reform in England will continue to be, as it has been in the past, by act of Parliament. It will, if the claim made at the beginning of this study is just, continue to follow a line of progress of its own, largely independent of political parties. Reform is brought about by forces more powerful and more far-reaching than party plans or exigencies.

As parties now stand, if the Conservatives return to power the progress of reform will probably be slow. They are largely the party of the status quo. If it is conceivable that the Liberal party should again obtain a majority in Parliament, it can only be on some such basis as that of the "Liberal Inquiry into Britain's Industrial Future," on the title page of which the word "Liberal" might then not improperly be crossed out, and the word "Socialist" written in. If the present Labour party achieves power as well as office, it stands committed to a program of extensive reform based on thorough-going socialist principles.

There is just one other possibility; that by sloth-fulness of other parties in reform, by neglect of the dissemination of knowledge, by economic failure or by some great catastrophe, the Communist party should come into power and introduce its artificial and disastrous "dictatorship of the proletariat." But this is altogether unlikely; if it should occur it would set aside that orderly process of the evolution of reform which we have so far noted. Nothing is more marked in the series of events we have studied than the unbroken progress of reforming movements. They have marched on in their determined course. There have been no steps backward. There is every probability that reform will continue. The work of getting rid of barbarism, of injustice, of incapacity, of human weakness and suffering, the triumphs over our ignorance, may be scarcely yet begun. We are allowed by the astronomers a million million years before the constant decay of matter through radiation has reduced the temperature of the earth below the limit of man's capacity to live upon it. Even admitting that the later ages may be a period of inevitable decay, there are still, before that time comes, sufficient aeons for reform to have done its perfect work.